Hot Chocolate With God Devotional 2

Hot Chocolate With God Devotional 2

More Real Questions & Answers from Girls Just Like You

Camryn Kelly
with Jim and Erin Kelly

FaithWords

New York   Boston   Nashville

All Scripture quotations, unless otherwise indicated, are taken from the HOLY BIBLE, NEW INTERNATIONAL VERSION®. NIV®. Copyright © 1973, 1978, 1984 by Biblica, Inc™. Used by permission of Zondervan. All rights reserved.

Scripture quotations marked *The Message* are taken from *The Message*. Copyright © 1993, 1994, 1995, 1996, 2000, 2001, 2002 by NavPress Publishing Group. Used by permission. All rights reserved.

Scripture quotations marked (ESV) are from the HOLY BIBLE, ENGLISH STANDARD VERSION® (ESV®). Copyright © 2001 by Crossway, a publishing ministry of Good News Publishers. All rights reserved. ESV Text Edition: 2011

FaithWords
Hachette Book Group
1290 Avenue of the Americas
New York, NY 10104

www.faithwords.com

Printed in the United States of America

WOR

First Edition: October 2014
10 9 8 7 6 5 4 3 2 1

FaithWords is a division of Hachette Book Group, Inc.
The FaithWords name and logo are trademarks of Hachette Book Group, Inc.

The Hachette Speakers Bureau provides a wide range of authors for speaking events. To find out more, go to www.hachettespeakersbureau.com or call (866) 376-6591.

The publisher is not responsible for websites (or their content) that are not owned by the publisher.

Library of Congress Cataloging-in-Publication Data

Kelly, Camryn, 1999-
    Hot chocolate with God devotional. #2: more real questions & answers from girls just like you / Camryn Kelly with Jill and Erin Kelly. —First Edition.
        pages cm
    ISBN 978-1-4555-2855-4 (hardcover)—ISBN 978-1-4555-5517-8 (ebook) 1. Girls—Religious life—Juvenile literature. 2. Preteens—Religious life—Juvenile literature. I. Title.
    BV4551.3.K433 2014
    248.8'2—dc23
    2013049830

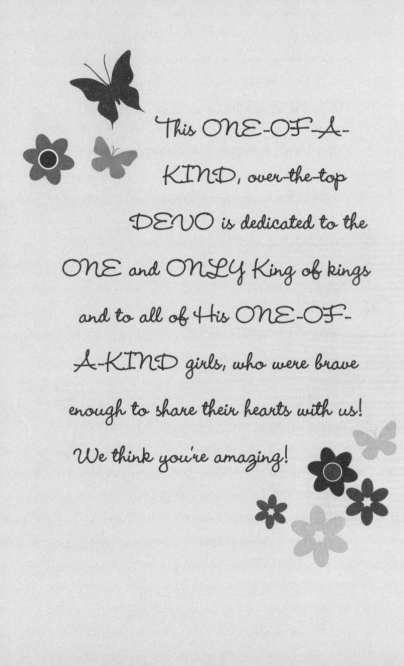

This ONE-OF-A-KIND, over-the-top DEVO is dedicated to the ONE and ONLY King of kings and to all of His ONE-OF-A-KIND girls, who were brave enough to share their hearts with us! We think you're amazing!

This unlike-any-other devotional belongs to:

....

Don't let anyone look down on you because you are young, but set an example for the believers in speech, in life, in love, in faith and in purity.

1 Timothy 4:12

Thank you...

First, to Jesus—Anything that actually matters is a gift from You. Thank You for creating *HCWG* and for allowing us to be a part of what You're doing to spread **Your** story! Please help us as we live each day to know and love YOU more! And please bless every single girl who reads this book.

GOD'S GIRLS—To the hundreds of girls who shared their questions with us through the *HCWG* website. WOW! Thank you! We trust that God will bless you in ways that only He can! You rock! Luv you!

My girls...Ally, Bailey, Kiley, Gabby, Olivia, and Alyssa—Thank you all so much for helping out with the **Cam Clips**! It was fun, but I know it wasn't always easy. Love you all so much!

Rick Kern—*Hot Chocolate With God Devotional #2*, book number five, and still going strong. You're such a blessing, Mr. Kern! Thank you for shining His light in everything you do.

The FaithWords team—Jana, thank you for always being so patient and good to us. We've been so blessed to work with you through all the HCWG everything. The best is yet to come! ☺

Team Wolgemuth—Thank you for all that you have done to help Team Kelly share the love of Jesus! We thank God for all of you.

To my mom and my sister, Erin—Last, but certainly not least...Sissy and Mommie...I can't believe we're here. The last HCWG book (hopefully not ☺). God continues to show us in so many ways how He has blessed HCWG. And we know He deserves all the credit—period. I LOVE YOU SO MUCH!

Contents

My Heart to Yours...

Sometimes I just don't know what to say. *What? Um, excuse me, you're writing this book, so you better figure out what you're going to say to these girls.* Ugh! Exactly! I know.

I guess what I'm trying to say is that I hope more than anything that God will do all the talking. Ya see, we could write and write and pray and write some more, but if all you get out of this is just us, just the Kelly girls and what we have to share with you...well, that would stink. It would. Why?

Well, because we're a work in progress, just like you.

We're trying to learn and live for Jesus, just like you.

We make mistakes, just like you.

We need God big-time, just like you.

Without God in all of this, just forget it. *Wow, Camryn, you're so encouraging.* LOL. Hey, I'm just trying to get us started on the right foot. (And just curious here, what is the right foot—the left or the right foot? Yeah! Whatever!)

We really, really want God to do what only God can do in your heart as you read this book. We pray that He will just absolutely blow you away. It can happen. And not because we want it to, but because God longs to make Himself known to you. He wants to talk to you! He wants to show you what He's like so you can know and love Him more. Because here's the deal: when you know and love Him more, you will live for Him.

Whoa, so maybe I'm getting a little deep. Let me just say it as simply as I know how: *Girl, God is crazy about you, and He wants to do something very exciting in and through your life.*

Yes, **YOUR LIFE!**

He wants to add His "extra" to your so-called ordinary life to make it extraordinary. Why? Because God is out of this world. Literally. He is beyond our understanding. He didn't create you just because. No, He has a perfect purpose designed for your life.

YOUR LIFE!

Seriously, please try to get your mind and heart wrapped around this truth:

GOD IS CRAZY ABOUT YOU! HE WANTS TO DO SOMETHING VERY EXCITING IN AND THROUGH YOUR LIFE!

This is your time!
This is our time!
This is *His* time!

Time to be who God created you to be.

But in order to be who He created you to be, you need to know who He is first.

When we know Him—not just know about Him, but when we really *know* Him—everything else falls into place. Now don't get me wrong, this doesn't mean that everything will go the way we want it to or that everything that happens will make sense. No, in fact God works in ways that we don't always understand. He's God!

In getting to know Him more, we learn who we are and who we're meant to be. This is it...

It's why we're here.

It's why you shared your hopes, fears, dreams, and tears with us.

It's why we wrote this book.

To **KNOW HIM** more!

To know Him and make Him known!

Oh yeah! That's a good one! I'm pretty sure I heard my mom say that last line a few hundred times. ☺

So let's do this. Together!

The questions you read here are real.

Real questions from real girls!

With answers from us—my sister, Erin (the wiser one), me (the fun, "learning to know and love Jesus every single day" girl), and the

Real God. What? THE REAL GOD! Yes, the One who sits on His throne watching over all the earth and heavens—that God!

This book is made up of the things that matter—everything that MATTERS to you, in your life, right now.

IF IT MATTERS TO YOU—IT MATTERS TO GOD!

Bam!

This is **GOOD NEWS**!

And…if it matters to God, it should matter to you!

Oh yeah! High five! I'm on a roll now. LOL!

God cares about everything that's going on in your life right now. Even the things that you think are no big deal—He cares about those very things too. Why? Because **HE LOVES YOU!**

Erin and I are so excited for you and trust that God is going to do immeasurably more than all we could ever ask, pray, or imagine in your life.

Are you ready?

I'll be honest with you, I'm sort of, like, freaking out.

So let's start this off with a quick prayer—okay?

Heavenly Father...

Here we are! You created us. You see us. You know us more than we know ourselves. Thank You for what You already have planned for us as we go about this devotional adventure. Help this to not be just another book that we read. Lord,

please open our minds and hearts so we can hear You speaking to us.

Please, Lord, help us to know and love You more so we can bring the message of who You are to the world. We pray that this devotional experience would be unforgettable because of what You did in our hearts and lives. In Jesus' Name we pray...

And all God's girls said...AMEN!

Okay...here we go!

Love you,

Camryn ("Cam")

Get the Devo 411 Before You Have Fun...

So...there are a few important things I need to tell you before we go all in. You might already know what I'm about to share because, well, you and I have some history, girl. This isn't your first *HCWG* rodeo. LOL! Oh my! Please tell me I'm not the only one laughing right now. While I go laugh my head off, please make sure you read the 411 below. If you don't know what 411 means, I'll tell you—it's the number version for "For Your Information." Yeah! Who came up with that anyway? I mean I get 911—sort of—but 411? Anyway, read on and I'll see you in a minute.

1. First of all, let's get one thing perfectly clear—GOD is FOR YOU! And so are we (meaning my sister, my mom, and me)! God has a plan and purpose for your life. If you're holding this book, there's something awesome in the midst of these pages that God wants to say to you. I'm SERIOUS! Don't just read this book. Stop. Listen. And ask

God to speak to your heart. I promise—He will! He will speak right to you. How do I know this? Well, because I know that God loves you and He wants to use this book to help you know Him better. You'll see!

2. We're going online, girl! YES! Throughout this book I will encourage you to go to the *Hot Chocolate With God* website (www.hotchocolatewithgod.com) to view **Cam Clips**. When you see a Cam Clip, there will be a special code word next to it that you will need when you log in to the website. At the Cam Clips section of the website you will type in these special codes to view the very cool, suppa videos. You cannot view these videos without typing in the code exactly as you see it in the book—so make sure you type the words in all uppercase. No worries, you'll get the hang of it. (What does that even mean? "The hang of it"—so weird.)

3. VERY IMPORTANT! ALWAYS, ALWAYS, ALWAYS ask your parents before you get on the Internet. It's so IMPORTANT that you always, in every way, protect your heart. The *HCWG* website is a safe place—

so when you're there don't go surfing anywhere else because you don't know what's out there. Okay? Got that?!

4. **Devo #2** contains something amazing called **Sweet Truths**. These incredible passages come from God's Word—the Bible. Here's the deal: We could tell you all this stuff that's true, but God's Word is TRUTH. Therefore, what He says is all that really matters. People always say, "How does God talk to us?" Well, the answer is through His Word…through HCWG **Sweet Truths**. Amazing! Yeah, I know! So let's GO!

5. Last, but very important—we decided to do something different this time around as far as how *HCWG Devo #2* is organized. Some devotionals are an everyday sort of thing—like each day is dated. I'm sure you know what I mean. **Devo #1** was organized by topics, like friends, family, God—that sort of thing. Well, for **Devo #2** we decided to put it all out there and just trust that whatever God wants to speak into your heart at that very moment—He will. Now that's a lot of TRUST. Yeah, it is. Because we have received thousands of questions through the website, we had a hard time deciding

which ones to use. Once again, we prayed about it and decided to pick the questions we felt God wanted us to share. Maybe you'll end up reading one question per week, so to speak! Or maybe, like some girls, you'll use this book as a group study. SOOO COOL! Whatever you choose to do, we know that God will be with you. It's all yours...and you're all HIS! So go for it!

SWEET Devos All About...

WORRY, LOVE, courage, being popular, feeling forgotten, when my parents always fight, BETRAYAL, bad influences, loneliness, confusion, being shy, real Christianity, gifts from GOD, LOVE, reading and understanding the Bible, prayer, MONEY, embarrassing moments, feeling hopeless, WAITING, mean girls, MIRACLES, divorce, being made fun of, when bad things happen, sharing your faith, DIFFICULT PEOPLE, how to be happy, RELIGION, identity—who am I, friendship issues, temptations, JESUS, social media, CHARACTER, trust, forgiveness, dealing with change, CONFIDENCE, back-talking, bad decisions, PERFECTION, selfish or selfless, body issues, BOYS, how can I make a difference in this world, dealing with doubt, death, PEOPLE PLEASER, gossip, respect...

What is the true definition of love?
—monkeyluver41

Cam: Love is Justin Bieber. JUST KIDDING! Okay, for all you girls who are not JB fans—just go with me here, because you have to admit the kid is gorgeous. And his mom loves Jesus, so let's give him a break, people. Again, just kidding! But we could pray for him...not a bad idea, ya know?

So what about love? I used to think love was just a feeling—like I love my family. I do think love is about how you feel toward special people, but it's more than just a feeling. It's the way you treat people. Jesus told us that we should love our enemies (Matthew 5:44). How is this even possible if love is just a feeling? Exactly.

Love is an action. It's how you treat people—the way you would want them to treat you. It's about putting the cares and needs of others before your own. Seriously, this is impossible without Jesus. We can't sincerely love others, including our enemies, without the love of Jesus in us. I'm going to let Sissy take it from here because I'm getting all serious and she's better at explaining the deeper things. Besides, I'm thinking about Justin Bieber now and need a short snack break. (Barbecue chips and cranberry-grape juice here I come! Hey, feel free to take a snack break too if you need one. Sometimes a girl has to do what a girl has to do! Are you feelin' me here?)

Erin: Well, apparently we lost Cam for a bit. I just have to laugh because she seriously needs her snacks—and her Justin Bieber. Oh boy, I've been praying for her.

So let's talk about love. It's impossible to know what real love is unless you know the love of God through Christ. What I just said may sound sort of radical or extreme, but it's true. "God is love" (1 John 4:8). In fact the rest of that verse makes a few things about love very clear—"Anyone who does not love does not know God, because God is love." WOW! So if I understand what this says, and I'm pretty sure I do—if I don't love others (including my enemies) then I don't know God. If God is love, then everything else that we think love is…is not really true love. The world tries to tell us what love is, but God—the One who is love—is the only true source of all love.

I don't want to keep talking in circles, so the bottom line is this—if you want to know what real love is—look at God. One more thing: There are many verses about love in the Bible. This **Sweet Truth** is one of my favorites.

Sweet Truth

**Love never gives up.
Love cares more for others
than for self.
Love doesn't want what it doesn't have.
Love doesn't strut,
Doesn't have a swelled head,
Doesn't force itself on others,
Isn't always "me first,"
Doesn't fly off the handle,
Doesn't keep score of sins of others.
Doesn't revel when others grovel,
Takes pleasure in the
flowering of truth,
Puts up with anything,
Trusts God always,
Always looks for the best,
Never looks back,
But keeps going to the end.**
—1 Corinthians 13:4–8
(The Message)

The world tries to tell us what love is, but God—the One who is love—is the only true source of all love!

So let's plaster hearts all over the house—or maybe just your bedroom. Come on, let's make a bunch of cutout hearts and write parts of the verse we shared inside the hearts and then tape them all over the place as a reminder. Yes, your friends might think you're celebrating Valentine's Day, but then you can share God's love with them when they ask you why all the hearts. So COOL! I know you know what to do, but just in case you don't, watch this **Cam Clip**. You'll LOVE it!

CAM CLIPS CODE: HEARTS

I've hit a hard time in my life because my parents just got divorced. I feel like it's all my fault!
—Melaney

Cam: Although I don't personally know what it's like to experience divorce, my best friends in the whole world do. Unfortunately, their parents don't get along at all, so their situation is what you would call an ugly divorce. As if divorce could ever possibly be pretty. I see how much pain divorce has caused my BFFs. It's awful. But I have also watched my friends turn to God time and time again. In fact, their faith is strong today because instead of turn-ing to their earthly father who is never there for them, they turn to God, their Heavenly Father—who is always there for them, no matter what. And He's there for you too. What God can do for you goes far beyond what your earthly parents could ever do for you.

 I don't know if the divorce situation in your life will ever get easier, but I do believe that God will show you one day at a time how to trust Him more in the middle of it all. He will help you have joy even when you're sad. I know this sounds crazy, but God can and will do this in your life if you turn to Him.

Erin: First and foremost, God sees you. He knows what's going on in your life and cares about you more than you can comprehend. Your parents' divorce is NOT your fault. Please hear me when I tell you that what's happening between your parents has nothing to do with you. I know it's hard to believe because you want to find a reason something like this would happen to your family. When a family gets torn apart by divorce there's got to be someone to blame—right? Well, the truth is that the bigger enemy in this is the evil one. He wants to kill, steal, and destroy families and people—especially God's family.

But here's the good news. God can take what's ugly and make it beautiful. I'm sure what you're experiencing right now doesn't feel very beautiful. But God is still God, and He can do the impossible. He has a plan for you in the midst of all that you're going through. Maybe He wants you to see and know that He's trustworthy and faithful—even when your whole life seems like it's falling apart. God is good all the time. He will take what the enemy meant for evil and use it in your life for good! You'll see!

God is still God and He can do the impossible!

"Don't you see, you planned evil against me but God used those same plans for my good, as you see all around you right now." —Genesis 50:20 *(The Message)*

What would you do if you thought you could trust your friend and she betrayed you? I want to forgive her, but I don't think I'll ever be able to trust her again. Do you think our friendship is over? —Shelby

Cam: Ouch! Ugh, why does stuff like this have to happen between friends? I just don't get it. Don't you wish things could be great all the time without all the ups and downs? But here's the deal—no one is perfect, so when you put two imperfect people together you're going to have issues on both sides. That's why we all need Jesus. He created relationships. He created you, your friends, everything—so He knows what it takes to make friendships work and grow.

It's complicated and hard work. And I don't think there are any easy answers for this because we all blow it now and then. Only God really knows if your friendship is over.

Of course this would be sad and very hard, but maybe God has a different plan for both of you. You're going to have to pray and talk to Him. You're also going to have to decide if you can trust your friend—this one is huge because it's almost impossible to have a close relationship with someone you don't trust. However, God can do what seems impossible to you—He can restore your friendship. In fact, He's God, so He can make your friendship even stronger through all of this. What a cool testimony that would be.

One more thing. If your friend apologized, you must forgive her, because that's where getting your relationship back on track starts. And forgiveness is also the first step to earning trust back all the way around. Forgiveness is a must—even when it doesn't make sense, even when it hurts, even when you don't want to forgive.

Erin: This might be sort of deep, but forgiveness and trust are two different things. It's not necessarily wrong to mistrust someone, even if you forgive her. Love is unconditional and a forgiving attitude is uncondi- tional, but trust is conditional. Relationships need things like boundaries, respect, and trust, to name a few. There are people that you know you can still have as friends but you're not close with them

Forgiveness is a must—even when it doesn't make sense, even when it hurts, even when you don't want to forgive.

because you know you can't trust them—they don't have your back. Do you know what I mean? It's like you can still hang out with them, but trusting these people with your heart and the really important things in your life is not happening.

Jesus was betrayed by one of His closest friends. He understands what you're going through, and He longs to help you work through all of your relationship ups and downs.

He knows what's best for you and your friend.

You might not trust your friend, but you can choose to trust God with her. This is huge! If we can get this and put it into practice, it will help all of our relationships.

Press on, girl, and remember what a true and best friend you have in Jesus!

A friend loves at all times.
—Proverbs 17:17

I have a hard time talking to people about God. I would really like to, but I get scared and embarrassed. Do I have to tell people about Jesus? I would really like to share about Him. But I'm afraid I won't get accepted. —Halia

Cam: When I was younger, I was crazy bold about sharing my faith in Jesus. In fact, it didn't matter where we were or what we were doing, I would ask my mom if I could tell the people around us about Jesus. Oh my, I still can't believe I was so fearless. I remember one time we were at this arts and crafts place where you paint pottery and stuff. We were just having fun and everything, but I was determined to find out if the lady in charge of the place knew Jesus. I kept asking my mom to ask her. Because I was so relentless Mom finally gave in, and I ended up asking the lady if she had ever asked Jesus into her heart. I'm laughing right now just thinking about it.

Unfortunately, I'm not as brave as I used to be. I don't

know if it's because I'm scared or what. When Erin's done sharing we need to pray about this. Seriously, if Jesus is God and if knowing Him changes everything, we should want to share our faith all the time, with everyone. No matter what!

Erin: When Cam was a little girl, she really was courageous. It didn't matter what people thought or what they said, she just wanted them to know Jesus. We were both young, but I can still remember how bold Cam was. I don't know what happened with her Jesus spunk. Maybe, like you, she's afraid of being rejected or made fun of. Regardless of what might happen, Jesus is worth stepping out of your comfort zone. He's worth the risk. The more you know Him, the more on fire you become, and the more you can't help but tell people about Him.

There are so many stories of courageous faith in the New Testament. In fact, I could fill the rest of this book with story after story of how ordinary people did extraordinary things for the sake of sharing the Good News—the Gospel. The story of Jesus is the only story that matters. You and I have a story, but our story is only worth telling if it's part of the greater story—His story. This is how I tell people about God. I tell them my story, my testimony of how I came to recognize my need for a Savior and how Jesus rescued me from a life filled with sin, a life without my only Hope. Be encouraged. As Christians, we have a testimony, and it's meant to be shared. God will give you the opportunity and courage to share what He has done in your life. Remember, the most powerful story is His story, and He will give you everything you need to tell people what they need to know.

 **Preach the word; be prepared in season and out of season; correct, rebuke and encourage—with great patience and careful instruction.**—2 Timothy 4:2

 Here's a GREAT idea to share the Gospel in a very fun and easy way. Get sticky notes and write out Bible verses that will speak to someone's life (like friends or family members). Remember to be wise about the Scriptures you choose. THEN...

(are you ready?) hide them all over—in underwear drawers, shoes, books, cars, pots and pans— you get the idea.

In fact, you can personalize them too, like insert your mom's, dad's, and friends' names to help them understand the meaning better. Here's an example of John 3:16: "For God so loved *(mother's name goes here instead of the words 'the world')* that He gave His one and only Son, that *('if she would believe' goes here instead of 'whosoever believes')* in Him, *(her name again)* shall not perish but have eternal life."

Got it? Have fun!

Okay…well, we decided to go and do what we're talking about. Let's talk to people about God.

CAM CLIPS CODE: GOD TALK

Some people in my family are just hard to be around. What should I do, since it seems like they'll never change? —*billy jo*

Cam: I was going to joke around and say that I know how you feel because I have an older sister. But she's amazing. If anything, I'm the one that might be difficult to be around from time to time. Oh boy! The truth hurts. So here's the deal: People can't just change. It's not like we have in us what it takes to change, to be different. God is the only one capable of changing His children. He's the only one who knows exactly what we need. He even knows the number of hairs on your head (Matthew 10:30).

So to answer your question—what should you do?—well, let go and let God do what only He can do. Of course pray—pray for the people you're talking about and for yourself—that God would help you to love your family no matter how much they drive you crazy.

Erin: What if God has placed certain people in your life so you would learn, grow, and change, so maybe you would become more like Jesus? It's not an accident or a mistake that your family is together. In fact, God determined the exact place you would be born and where you would live (Acts 17:26), so you can be sure that He handpicked the very people in your family—even the ones who are hard to be around.

What if God did this so you would depend more on Him and less on your own ability and strength? What if the very things that bother you about other people are the things in you that need to change? Okay, I might be going a bit too far, but maybe you need to take some time to think about what I'm saying. In fact, I need to think about what I'm saying; we all do. You're not the only one who has to live with difficult people. At the end of the day (and the beginning and every minute), God wants us to love Him and

> **What if the very things that bother you about other people are the things in you that need to change?**

love others. The more we love Him, the more we will love others. It would be impossible to love anyone without God first choosing to love us. Through His love in you, you can love the people around you in ways you never dreamed possible.

Sweet Truth

Live in harmony with one another. Do not be proud, but be willing to associate with people of low position. Do not be conceited. Do not repay anyone evil for evil. Be careful to do what is right in the eyes of everyone. If it is possible, as far as it depends on you, live at peace with everyone. —Romans 12:16-18

Why is it so hard to fit in? What do I do when no matter what I try to do I just cannot get into the popular group? I feel forgotten. Every time I try to stand out I get teased, and people say I don't fit in and that I should leave the school and never come back. What should I do? *—karrie*

Cam: First of all, you're NOT forgotten. Absolutely not!

GOD loves you and will never forget about you! I can't remember where I heard it, but there's a quote that I think is perfect for you. Here it is: "Why do you try so hard to fit in when you were born to stand out?" Oh yeah! Bam! Now that's an awesome quote. I should tweet it. (Um, I was just thinking that you might think tweeting is like pretending that you're a bird or something. LOL! No, tweeting is putting messages on a social media network called Twitter. If you don't understand what I'm talking about, you might want to ask an adult to explain it.) Anyway, Erin will take over while I go tweet that cool quote. Be right back! ☺

Erin: While Cam is tweeting I'm going to dig a little deeper with this one. I think it's natural to want to fit in, be a part of a group of people, be a member of a family, find a place where you feel like you can be yourself and feel loved. These needs are very real and natural. God made us to do life together—like one big family—His family. He created you to be part of a bigger family beyond the one you live with. In His family, you do fit in—whether you feel like you do or not. God created you exactly how He wanted you to be so you would fit perfectly into His family. He wants you to be the girl He made so you can display His glory like no one else can—because you're you and no one else on the face of the earth can be you. So listen…YOU FIT IN, because God made you and that's all that matters. It doesn't matter what anyone else says or thinks. You fit in perfectly in the family of God. When you believe this powerful truth it will change the way you see yourself and the world.

 **Long, long ago He decided to adopt us into His family through Jesus Christ. (What pleasure He took in planning this!)** —Ephesians 1:5 *(The Message)*

Someone very close to me is doing drugs, and I'm begging God on my knees asking Him to help this person stop, but it's not working. What should I do? Am I praying wrong? —*Girl in Need*

Cam: I'm so sorry, and I will pray too. It's like I can almost feel your broken heart and your sorrow. I have to say right from the start, if you're praying for someone to stop doing drugs, you're not praying wrong. God knows your heart and sees your pain. Even though you don't see the results yet, your prayers are being heard and God is at work, even when it seems like He's not.

Don't give up! Don't stop praying!

Don't give up! Don't stop praying! I know you wish your prayers were answered yesterday, but God has His own timetable. He has to move in this person's heart so he/she will WANT to quit using drugs. Only God can do this.

Again, NO, you're not praying wrong. The only way it would be wrong is if it was insincere or if you were trying to get God to do what you want Him to do rather than His perfect will (LOL...as if this could ever happen—He's GOD!). Let's see what my wise older sister thinks.

Erin: Wow, I'm really sorry and sad with you. It sounds like you love this person so much that you're literally praying on your knees. The fact that you would bend down and get before God in this way says so much about you, your love and concern for this person, as well as your reverence and respect for God. It sounds like your heart is in the right place, and therefore your prayers are reaching the heart of the Father.

Keep praying and loving. The way we treat someone says so much more than our words and prayers ever can. So love this person in your life like Jesus loves him/her, with all the imperfections, hang-ups, and rebellion—remember Jesus' love for us led Him to the cross to die for us when we were full of sin, before we ever surrendered our lives to Him. Love with that kind of love and get creative...maybe hide notes telling this person what he/she means to you, or with Scripture verses on them, in a jacket pocket or a purse (not if this is a guy—of course ☺). Be creative—let him/her know he/she is loved and treasured whether using drugs or not, PERIOD. That kind of love supported by prayer is powerful stuff. And lastly, keep praying!

Sweet Truth

The prayer of a righteous person is powerful and effective. —James 5:16b

My parents don't really like this boy I'm talking to, but I really like him and he treats me like a princess. I don't want to lose him, but I don't want to dishonor my mama and dad. What would you do? —Abby

Cam: I'm just wondering, did you ever ask your parents why they don't like this boy? Your mom and dad love you and want the best for you, so I'm sure they have some very good reasons as to why they aren't thrilled with this kid you're talking to. When you say "talking" what do you actually mean? Just talking like friends, or as my sister would say, "talk-talking," which usually means that you really like the boy and you're close to dating? Regardless, Mom and Dad come before the boy *always—no matter what.*

Erin: I absolutely agree with Camryn—your parents and their rules and instructions for you must come first. No exceptions or excuses. Clearly God thinks it's of utmost importance that you and I honor and respect our parents; He included them in the Ten Commandments (see the next **Sweet Truth**). Yes,

> If it matters to God, it should matter to you.

the big ten! If it matters to God, it should matter to you. If your parents don't want you to talk to this boy anymore and you choose to honor their wishes, God will bless you. If you end up losing this boy's friendship as a result, God must have a better plan for your life. His plan would never contradict His Word. In other words, He would never want you to dishonor your parents for some boy.

One more thought for you. Please know that what I'm going to say next is filled with as much grace and love as I can extend through words—no boy can ever treat you like the princess you truly are because there's only one King and Prince. Stay with me for a minute. We're all fallen human beings. No matter how good this boy treats you, he can never satisfy the deepest longings in your heart. Jesus is the only one who knows exactly what you need. He is the fulfillment of your every need. This boy, no matter how hard he tries, no matter how cool he is and how good he treats you, he still needs Jesus—just like you do.

Sweet Truth

Honor your father and your mother, as the LORD your God has commanded

you, so that you may live long and that it may go well with you in the land the LORD your God is giving you. —Deuteronomy 5:16

Do you think social media is a good thing? Like Facebook, Instagram, and Twitter. I always check to see how many people like my pictures and all of that. Maybe I care too much what other people think. What do you think is the right thing to do about all of these things? —Reece

Cam: Oh boy! *Confession time…Lord, help me.* Okay, so you've been courageous enough to share your heart, so of course we will do the same. I went through a social media obsession. And it wasn't pretty. I was so concerned about the number of likes on my Instagram that I would call my grammie and ask her to like my pictures. Not only that, I would get on my mom's phone and like my pictures through her Instagram. It sort of got to be an obsession to the point where I would compare how many likes my pictures got with how many likes my friends got on their pictures. SO RIDICULOUS!

My mother eventually intervened. She sat me down and explained some very important things to me. First of all, she said that it doesn't matter whether or not anyone likes my pictures. Instagram is meant to be a fun way to share your life with other people through photos. If I like a picture and want to share it, that's all that matters. If people like my photo, great—but whether a lot of people like it or not doesn't determine whether or not it's a great picture. It's great because I like it. I hope I'm making sense. ☺

Another important thing to remember is this: *God cares about how I spend my time*. Sometimes (and trust me, I know this firsthand) Facebook and all that stuff can be a major distraction. So much so that we spend more time on our phones and computers than we do just hanging out with people face to face.

I really like social media, but I've had to learn (and continue to learn) how to use it and how not to let it use me. Oh yeah… that was deep. My sister is the deep thinker, so I'll let her take it from here.

GOD CARES ABOUT HOW I SPEND MY TIME!

Erin: You asked if we think social media is a good thing. But I'm wondering, is it a *God thing*? Because there's a lot of "good" in social media, but is it godly? Cam warned you that I go deep, so let's dive into this. We can share what we think is right all day long, but if our "good" doesn't line up with God, it doesn't really matter much, does it?

I think the various social media networks can be used for good—like connecting with people, sharing information, being a witness, etc. But you know as well as I do that the enemy lives to take what is good and use it for evil. Therefore, there's a lot of evil happening in the social media world. So I'm wondering, does that mean we're supposed to abandon all of it? I don't think so. But we have to be very careful and wise.

The awesome thing about all of this is that God knows what's going on. He knows how it all works. He knows the intentions of our hearts. He knows whether we will use social media for good or for evil. He KNOWS. And because He knows we can ask Him for help. We can seek wisdom from His heart in order to make godly choices. I think the **Sweet Truth** we share is perfect for this question. Wisdom is the answer. And God will freely give it to all who ask Him. So ask!

Sweet Truth

If any of you lacks wisdom, he should ask God, who gives generously to all without finding fault, and it will be given him.

—James 1:5

This is going to be fun and very informative and helpful. Here's what we're going to do—for one week (just seven days—you can do it!) we're going to keep track of how we spend our time. Don't you even think of rolling your eyes as if this were some sort of school project or something. Hello, you're with me so you know there's got to be more to this, and trust me there is.

Write down how much time you spend on the things you do every day. For instance, if you're in school from 8:15 a.m. to 3:00 p.m. (like I am) Monday through Friday, write it down. If you spend two hours on homework each day, write it down.

We've provided a very cool calendar for you, so make sure you have fun.

Sunday
_____

Monday
_____

Tuesday
_____

Wednesday
_____

Thursday
_____

Friday
_____

Saturday

When you've completed your calendar, PLEASE watch this **Cam Clip**.

♫ CAM CLIPS CODE: WISDOM

I spend a lot of time comparing myself to other girls, wishing I were prettier and stuff like that. How can I stop this? —*Pria*

Cam: Based on the hundreds of messages we've received through our website, a ton of girls struggle with exactly what you're talking about. They look at all the girls at school and those on magazine covers and other various media outlets, and they compare themselves in some way to what they see. We're so focused on what the world tells us that we think we have to measure up to a definition of beautiful that isn't really beautiful at all. It's sad but true.

Girl, I've struggled with this too. I'm taller than all my friends. A lot taller! So of course, I've wished I could be shorter. Ugh! I don't like not being content with exactly how God made me. In fact, worrying about it just makes me more aggravated. So what's the deal? What are we supposed to do? It's not like you can just turn off the switch in your mind that's telling you you're not good enough. I wish it were that easy, don't you?!

Erin: Cam, it's not easy, but it's possible. It's possible to change the way you think. WHAT? Yes, and when you change the way you think, you change the way you act. It's called renewing your mind. (Check out the **Sweet Truth**.) Replacing the lies that constantly bombard you with the truth that sets you free. Free to be all that God created you to be.

Listen, girls, you don't need more self-confidence, because all that will do is keep you focused on yourself. What you need is God confidence—confidence in who God is and who He says you are.

You are fearfully and wonderfully made. God created you exactly how He wanted you to be. There is no one else on the face of the earth like you. No one can be you. When you fix your eyes on the One who created you and knows you, it changes how you see yourself and others. The only way you're ever going to be able to stop comparing yourself to other girls is by thanking God for who He is and how He made you. All of

> When you fix your eyes on the One who created you and knows you, it changes how you see yourself and others!

this comparing and wishing you were prettier drains your brain. It's a waste of the precious time God has given you each day. It's a distraction from all that God designed you to be.

We like both versions of this **Sweet Truth**, so we decided to share both with you. Check it out!

Do not conform any longer to the pattern of this world, but be transformed by the renewing of your mind. Then you will be able to test and approve what God's will is—His good, pleasing and perfect will. —Romans 12:2

Embracing what God does for you is the best thing you can do for Him. Don't become so well-adjusted to your culture that you fit into it without even thinking. Instead fix your attention on God. You'll be changed from the inside out. —Romans 12:2 *(The Message)*

Every minute of every day everyone in my house is negative, angry, sad, and grumpy. To see people feeling and being like this also makes me so sad. I can't live like this anymore. PLEASE HELP! —AJ

Cam: Wow! This is a hard situation, but it's not bigger than God. I think everyone comes up against some sort of negativity in life. It seems like there's always something or someone trying to bring us down. The first thing I noticed, though, is that the discouraging things you mentioned: the anger, negativity, and sorrow surrounding you—well, they are all unacceptable to you. You have an understanding of what a healthy home should look like. You can see that the way things are is not how they should be. That's really a good thing; it shows you aren't just ignoring everything, pretending all this is okay. And I think your reaction is good too—it should make you sad because you love your family and want joy-filled lives for them and for yourself, not all the negative stuff, anger, and sorrow.

One bit of advice I would pass on is that you are not responsible for anyone else's actions or attitudes, no matter how much you care about them. You can't live anyone's life but yours, and even though you may love them so much, you can't make their choices for them. What you can do is make your own decisions—live as close to God as you can. You can choose to walk according to the Word of God and trust Him with everything else— kind of like what my mom says, "You do your best and let God take care of the rest."

Erin: As hard as it may be sometimes, be a light, even in the darkness. Separate yourself. Be determined to live in the light and give your loved ones to Jesus. Pray constantly for them, share the Word of God, and though it may not happen overnight, just as Paul and Silas prayed and worshiped God in prison and the prisoners heard them, the same may happen in your family. They may be in the darkness of their anger, sadness, and negativity, but when you live your life in the light of God's peace, joy, and hope, you will have a powerful effect on them.

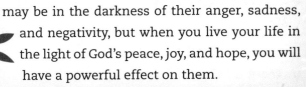

As hard as it may be sometimes, be a light, even in the darkness!

One thing I know about darkness; it cannot defeat light. Check out Acts 16:25–32; as those two men of God worshiped from that cold, dark prison, the doors burst open and their chains fell off. I really believe the

chains of frustration and sorrow you feel will fall off, and the negativity will lose its power over you—and hopefully your family—as you walk in the light.

One more thing, and this is just a practical thing you can do. We all tend to be influenced by our peer groups—the people we spend the most time with, like our friends—so spend more time "in the light" with encouraging friends. Get involved in church activities that are both fun and helpful. That way you can encourage one another and learn more about the Lord, His Word, and how to strengthen your relationship with Him. I think the **Sweet Truth** we picked is a good one to memorize regarding all that we've been talking about. Shine on, girl!

But if we walk in the light, as He is in the light, we have fellowship with one another, and the blood of Jesus, His Son, purifies us from all sin. —1 John 1:7

I'm so worried about my sister. She's been doing a lot of bad things. It's like she doesn't care about her family and is just neglecting God and us. It seems like she only cares about her friends, boys, and her phone. I can't stop thinking about the bad things she might do, and I just stress about her every day. I can't even enjoy the special things in life without worrying. I can't explain how much I worry and it's ruining my life! PLEASE HELP! —bekah

Cam: Ugh! I hate stress and worry. Ya know what, your sister may not realize it now, but she's crazy blessed to have a sister like you who cares so much. Look, the first thing that comes to mind is often the hardest: **PRAY!** I can't help but think of Ephesians 6:12: "For our struggle is not against flesh and blood, but against the rulers, against the authorities, against the powers of this dark world and against the spiritual forces of evil in the heavenly realms." Even though your sister is doing a lot of bad things, the battle is against those "spiritual forces of evil in the heavenly realms" that are influencing her choices.

Praying is a fight, and it's not easy for many reasons (that verse actually calls it a "struggle"). Our minds are constantly being bombarded with things we have to do, or crazy distractions like the dog barking, thoughts of Justin Bieber or One Direction, homework (oops, I suppose homework really shouldn't be considered a distraction), or even a grumbling tummy—those spiritual forces of evil do NOT want us praying against them, so they will try to get us thinking about and doing everything else but prayer! So get focused. Set aside some time every single day to pray for your sister. In fact, you can get started right here, right now! (Check out the next **Just Cool!**)

God does not want you to worry anymore!

Erin: Amen to that! The other thing is to lead a godly life—set an example. Remember what Cam shared with AJ in the question right before this one: you really can't make someone else's choices, but you can make your own. So if your sister is buying into the lie that her friends, phone, and boys will give her life meaning or bring her happiness, then living your life for Christ and finding true happiness, peace, and purpose as you walk in His Word will challenge her to reach for what's real.

It's hard to love so much and yet let go, but remember, it's the Holy Spirit's work to draw her back to a right relationship with Him. And remember one of the best things you can do is pray and **TRUST GOD**! Seriously! As hard as it is, God does not want you to worry anymore about this. In fact, you just might want to write the **Sweet Truth** down on a note card and put it where you'll read it often. Hopefully if you read it enough, your heart will receive the truth and you'll start trusting God to do what only He can do.

Sweet Truth **Do not be anxious about anything, but in everything, by prayer and petition, with thanksgiving, present your requests to God. And the peace of God, which transcends all understanding, will guard your hearts and your minds in Christ Jesus.** —Philippians 4:6-7

We love this verse SO, SO, SO MUCH that we decided to share two versions with you. Pick one or both and write them down. Read this verse every single day. Okay?

Don't fret or worry. Instead of worrying, pray. Let petitions and praises shape your worries into prayers, letting God know your concerns. Before you know it, a sense of God's wholeness, everything coming together for good, will come and settle you down. It's wonderful what happens when Christ displaces worry at the center of your life. —Philippians 4:6–7 *(The Message)*

WHY WAIT? Start praying right now for that person in your life who unfortunately is choosing to walk far from God. Prayer is powerful!

We'll get you started.

Heavenly Father,
You are the God who sees and knows everything. You know my fears, struggles, and tears. You see what's going on, and You're the only One who can help. You can do what seems impossible because You're God.

When we do questions in school after lessons, the teacher always calls on me. And then I tighten up and don't know what to say. I guess I'm just very shy. What can I do to open up a little? *—Kylie*

Cam: Well, talk about knowing how you feel—I'm a big fan of hiding in the back and letting others take the Q&As in class! I'd much rather be a fan cheering on a friend who's out front than a playmaker (what can I say, I come from a football family—"playmaker") when it comes to being called on or answering questions. Just ask my teachers, I'm usually the one sinking down in a chair or hiding behind the person half my size sitting in front of me! Trust me, that's a huge problem since I'm 5'11". Yeah, I'm tall, so trying to hide behind people can be a bit challenging to say the least. So I get it! Guess what's coming though—yep, a big "but"! So here you go, BUT...you totally blew me away and really challenged me just now—any idea why?

God is in your corner cheering you on!

Well, here it is: you didn't ask for ways to hide in the stands with the fans, you asked how to run the ball (football again—I know, I know. It's a daddy's girl thing; I'm working on it...) and THAT got me thinking!

Okay, we're in this together so here's what I'm thinking right now when it comes to shyness (and I actually looked over on my mom's office wall and, bam, this verse was right there—how about that for God's perfect timing? Oh yeah!) 2 Timothy 1:7, "For God hath not given us the spirit of fear; but of power, and of love, and of a sound mind." (Hey, quick thing. I need to find out what Bible version that is because the word "hath" just totally threw me off. Be back in a minute. Okay, got it. It's the King James Version. Yeah, no wonder.)

So the Apostle Paul was reminding Timothy that he had a gift from God and it was up to him to use it. But then he reminded him of something else: the fear that kept him from using his gift wasn't from God at all. It's the same with us shy people. Instead of letting our fear, shyness, or whatever you want to call it keep us from being brave, we need to remember that we have the power, love, and mind of Christ to use the gifts God has given us. So, my friend, **WE CAN DO THIS!**

Erin: Even if you're a "people person" there will still be intimidating and scary situations that demand that you step up and go for it. The best way I know to overcome the urge to give in to fear is to hold on to the truth that Jesus won't let you down—have faith in Him. I love Romans 8:31 (**Sweet Truth**) and hang on to it when, like David, I have to face a Goliath. It's a given in life that we have to face challenges bigger than we are, or we can't grow in faith. Our giants might not be nine feet tall like the monster David took out with his sling and a smooth stone, but whether we face personality traits like shyness or circumstances like bullies or math tests, we can still have faith in His faithfulness as we go up against them. God is in your corner cheering you on! YOU can because HE is—with you, faithful, good, trustworthy. He's everything you need!

Sweet Truth

What, then, shall we say in response to these things? If God is for us, who can be against us? —Romans 8:31

I rarely read my Bible and I forget to pray a lot. I feel like I can't be a true Christian because I'm not trying to follow Him each day. What do you think? —*Abi*

Cam: Great question, and it's awesome that you care enough about your relationship with God to ask it. Um, so you're reading this book and maybe you think that because my sister and I do things like the *HCWG* world that we are super Christians or something. SO NOT TRUE! In fact, and I can't even believe I'm going to say this, I struggle with reading my Bible and doing devotions and praying. You're not alone! I let way too many things steal my time with God. Your question is a reminder for me to get back to my **FIRST LOVE—JESUS**.

Before I say anything else, I need to say this...**GOD STILL LOVES YOU**. And He loves me. Even when we choose the things of this world instead of Him, His love for us never changes. Talk about Amazing Grace! Just the fact that God loves us anyway should move our hearts to spend more time with Him.

Following God is not just reading the Bible and praying. He doesn't love you any more if you know the Bible backward (which would be really cool) and forward, are reading it two hours a day (I wish), and memorizing twenty verses a week (well, that would be really hard)! That doesn't mean He doesn't want you to read His Word. Following the Word of God is following Jesus—living in the Word is living deeper in Jesus, in His love. And the better you know Him, the more you want to follow Him.

I could go n forever, but I'd better let Erin say what's in her heart. I'll be praying for you! ☺

Even when we choose the things of this world instead of Him, His love for us never changes.

Erin: Wow, I'm really impressed with this question, but it sounds to me like you might just be mixing up faith and works. I LOVE Ephesians 2:8–9, "For it is by grace you have been saved, through faith—and this is not from yourselves, it is the gift of God—not by works, so that no one can boast." We're all the same; we're saved by God's grace through believing in what Christ did, not by our good works, even works like praying or Bible reading.

It's not faith in Christ plus feeding the poor, or going to church, or reading the Word, or praying two hours a day...We're saved because of what Jesus did on the cross. End of story! On the other hand, the next verse in Ephesians says, "For we are God's handiwork, created in Christ Jesus to do good works, which God prepared in advance for us to do." God has a plan for us, a plan to do good, to show the world He's real and His kingdom is real—that He loves us. And any good we do is because we love Him and believe, NOT to prove to the world we're Christians. I know I'm sharing a lot here, so hang in there!

My advice is to focus on **BEING** in love with Jesus. If you invest in that, He will lead you into whatever works He wants you to DO (from Bible reading to loving your enemy—yes, your enemy)! Remember, the greatest commandment isn't "Do Christian things for God with all your heart, soul, mind, and strength!" It's...say it with me, "Love the Lord your God with all your heart and with all your soul and with all your mind and with all your strength" (Mark 12:30).

For it is by grace you have been saved, through faith—and this is not from yourselves, it is the gift of God—not by works, so that no one can boast. —Ephesians 2:8–9

My friend and I keep getting in fights. What should I do? I'm having a really hard time forgiving her. She hurt me big-time. I want to forgive her, but I keep thinking about what she did and it hurts. How can I forgive and move on?
—*Jaclyn*

Cam: I wish I didn't have any experience with this, but...I do. It's so weird because I love my friends and hate fighting, but it happens. Sometimes it's completely my fault, sometimes it's not. Sometimes it's because of jealousy or boys or attitudes, and oddly sometimes fights just happen and then you're like, "Why in the world are we even fighting anyway?" Can you relate?

I think disagreements are part of relationships. I wish they weren't, but you know as well as I do that no matter how much you love people there are times when you feel like you don't love them at all. I guess we have to try to remember that we're all imperfect people. We all make mistakes. We all fail from time to time. We all need Jesus.

Honesty, patience, and forgiveness are so important in a relationship. You need to be comfortable and honest enough to be able to talk to your friend. If there are issues, deal with them. Get them out. Tell it like it is. Forgive. And then give it to God. You can't control how your friend will respond. Also remember that this isn't a one-sided thing; you need to allow your friend to do the same with you. All relationships have ups and downs. In fact, sometimes the only way to get closer to a friend is to have a good brawl (minus the boxing gloves). Sometimes you just need to vent and cry and get it all out. But then forgive, hug, pray, and let God make you stronger. It's so important to try to see your friend's point of view and be understanding. Treat her the way you want to be treated, admit it if you're wrong, apologize, and be loving. You guys have to talk it out and resolve your differences. Remember, you're friends, not enemies!

One more thing. In fact, the most important thing—God keeps no record of wrongs. Did you just read what I wrote? God doesn't keep track. He doesn't keep a

We all make mistakes. We all fail from time to time. We all need Jesus.

list of all that we've done wrong. OH MY GOODNESS! If He doesn't keep a list, neither should we. It doesn't matter how many things you've done, GOD took care of it all through His Son, Jesus, on the cross. Because of this, we can live a life of forgiveness, because God has forgiven us. This is awesome, and I hope it encourages you to let God help you be the best friend you can be—for His glory and your good!

Erin: Wow! This is life-changing stuff we're talking about here. A great verse that comes to mind is Proverbs 27:17, "As iron sharpens iron, so one person sharpens another." Think about it: We're talking about smoothing out a relationship by rubbing the rough edges of our personalities against each other—as iron sharpens iron. So what you should do is try to talk about the constant fighting. Sometimes you just need a little time away from each other, other times you have to agree to disagree…Whatever it is, good relationships don't just happen—they take work.

Anything worth fighting for takes some fighting! Yeah, you can quote me on that. Of course we don't ever fight just for the sake of fighting. We fight for the sake of friendship because a godly friendship is worth fighting for. And remember, God is for you! He's cheering you both on as you seek Him in all things—especially your friendships.

Lastly, "a friend loves at all times" (Proverbs 17:17). At all times! Not some of the time. Not just when you're getting along. But absolutely at all times. Obviously, in order to "love at all times" you need Jesus.

 **Friends come and friends go, but a true friend sticks by you like family.** —Proverbs 18:24 *(The Message)*

 **"Be alert. If you see your friend going wrong, correct him. If he responds, forgive him. Even if it's personal against you and repeated seven times through the day, and seven times he says, 'I'm sorry, I won't do it again,' forgive him."** —Luke 17:3-4 *(The Message)*

Sweet Truth

Bear with each other and forgive whatever grievances you may have against one another. Forgive as the Lord forgave you. And over all these virtues put on love, which binds them all together in perfect unity.
—Colossians 3:13–14

Why do the bad things seem to be happening a lot more these days?
—meggy

Cam: It's hard not to notice that a lot of scary stuff has been going on in the world, and I agree, it does seem like bad things are happening a lot more these days. It could be that the time is drawing nearer to the return of the Lord. In fact, every day is one day closer. Right?

Now hear me, sister, I'm not up on the end times. In fact, I know very little about all of that. What I do know is this—Jesus is coming back, and before He does there will be a lot of evil happening on the earth. The Bible talks about the increase of wars, earthquakes, famines, and sicknesses before Jesus comes back. That's just the way He said it would be; for example, in Matthew 24:6–8 (*The Message*) He said, "'When reports come in of wars and rumored wars, keep your head and don't panic. This is routine history; this is no sign of the end. Nation will fight nation and ruler fight ruler, over and over. Famines and earthquakes will occur in various places. This is nothing compared to what is coming.'" Wow, that's kind of scary. But let's not forget WHO we belong to; and WHOSE side we're on—JESUS. He has already won the war because LOVE ALWAYS WINS.

We don't know when He'll return, only the Father does (Matthew 24:36), but I think the best answer I can give you is to not worry about it, just pray and trust God. Even though everything in the world seems like it's out of control, God is still God. He's still on His throne in heaven. He's still very much in control.

Erin: It's true that all these things have been happening throughout history, but they do seem to be growing in frequency and intensity. However, we

> Even though everything in the world seems like it's out of control, God is still God.

have to trust God to help us fulfill His plan for our lives and His kingdom. Whether He returns next week or next year or in a hundred years (of course we will be in heaven by then because I can't imagine any of us living past a hundred years old), we must trust Him, because the next heartbeat isn't promised to any of us. So we just have to live for Him and look to the promise of His coming just as He said, "When these things begin to take place, stand up and lift up your heads, because your redemption is drawing near" (Luke 21:28).

Knowing that every day is one day closer to seeing Jesus face to face should encourage us to live for Him…every minute of every day. Let's not let the concerns of this world distract us from what's true. For God so loved the world (even a very messed-up world like the one we live in) that He sent His One and Only Son, Jesus—to rescue and save us. Those who believe in Him will have abundant life now and an eternity in heaven. Despite all that's going on in your little world and the entire universe—God's got this all figured out!

Be still before the LORD and wait patiently for him; do not fret when people succeed in their ways, when they carry out their wicked schemes. —Psalm 37:7

Does God care about how I take care of my body? I mean, do I have to exercise and always eat good food? I love french fries and candy and not the best kinds of food. Am I supposed to care about all of this stuff?
—*Girl who loves food*

Cam: Oh boy. Well, girl, you and I have a lot in common. I love candy, barbecue and salt-and-vinegar chips, Lucky Charms, french fries, and most of the goodies out there. I think if they had Reese's Peanut Butter Cups when Jesus was here, He would've liked them. Don't you think? I can just see it now, Jesus and His twelve buddies sitting around a campfire passing around a bag of Doritos and Twizzlers.

I'll tell you this, I'm trying to eat better and exercise more. I'm trying to eat more fruits and vegetables (so hard to do) and play hoops as often as I can. I know it's important, but I'll be honest with you—I like how the unhealthy snacks taste. I can't just say good-bye to my barbecue chips forever—that would be torture. What I need to do, and maybe this will help you too, is exchange a bad snack for a healthy snack every other day. Yeah, and routine is good, so once we get into a better routine it will help us make even better decisions in the future. We're in this together, right?!

I know Erin has a lot to add, so before she shares, let me say one more thing. Listen, don't become obsessed with all this. Pray about it, start making some changes, and trust God. He wants you to take care of your body so you can live for Him. He will help you!

Erin: Yes, yes, yes, God cares about how you take care of your body. He cares about how you take care of every single thing He has given you. Your health is a gift from God. Your body needs healthy food to survive and thrive. Camryn is still in the process of learning this, and my parents continue to help her understand the importance of eating healthy and exercising.

I'm sure you've heard the saying, "Garbage in, garbage out." It's true. If you continue to put unhealthy foods and everything else (including what you watch and listen to), into your body, unhealthy junk will naturally come out. What I mean is that your body will automatically respond to how you treat it. If you put good and healthy things into your body, you will feel stronger, better, more alive. If you put nasty, processed junk in your body, you'll probably feel yucky, tired, and weak.

Now, I'm still learning about how to better care for my body. However, I can tell you from a few years of experience—eating better and exercising have changed my life for the better. Now when I choose to eat something unhealthy, or slack off on my workout routine, my body immediately responds—almost as if it's telling me to NOT do that ever again.

We honor God when we take care of our bodies.

Lastly, we honor God when we take care of our bodies. I don't know about you, but I want my life to radiate Christ. Of course I don't get it right every time, but God knows the motivations of my heart—and yours. He knows when we sincerely want to do everything we can in this life to please Him. If you want to make a few changes to better care for your body, ask God to help you. If you still don't care and want to go about it your way—ask God to help you to care. No matter what, He loves you and He's not going anywhere. He's ready to help when you're ready to change!

Sweet Truth

Do you not know that your body is a temple of the Holy Spirit, who is in you, whom you have received from God? You are not your own; you were bought at a price. Therefore honor God with your body. —1 Corinthians 6:19–20

Sweet Truth

So whether you eat or drink or whatever you do, do it all to the glory of God. —1 Corinthians 10:31

Cam: Erin has been at this healthy lifestyle stuff for a while. She's learned a lot, and if you really want to make some changes in how you eat, she has some great ways for you to get started. Check it out!

⨑CAM CLIPS CODE: HEALTHY BODY

A lot of kids in my school aren't Christians, and they judge me on my choices of music, TV shows, etc. What should I do? —Lex

Cam: Wow, my first thought is, "Excuse me, who are you to tell me what I can and cannot listen to or watch on TV?" And of course, our first thoughts or reactions in tough situations are not always the best or most godly. I wish my immediate response to everything that happens would be exactly how God would want me to respond. But I'm not in heaven yet, so that would be pretty much impossible. I'm still a work in progress and so are you. And God is still loving and gracious, and He forgives every time we come to Him with our messy attitudes.

It's never fun being judged. Hang in there, stay tough, and remember that Jesus said, "If the world hates you, keep in mind that it hated me first. If you belonged to the world, it would love you as its own. As it is, you do not belong to the world, but I have chosen you out of the world. That is why the world hates you" (John 15:18–19). So you, my friend, are in good company. If you're being put down because your music or TV picks aren't cool enough, it's not you, it's Christ in you that your classmates are rejecting. After all, I'm guessing that a desire to please Him is what determines what music and TV shows you choose. Pleasing Jesus over everyone else is more important than anything and everything. Besides, He knows what's going on. He sees and hears it all, so let God work in the hearts of these kids. He's the only true Judge anyway.

Pleasing Jesus over everyone else is more important than anything and everything.

Erin: I know it's hard to be judged and put down—especially when you're making godly or moral choices. But as Christians, we have set our hearts and minds on heavenly things, just as it tells us to in Colossians

3:1–2: "Since, then, you have been raised with Christ, set your hearts on things above, where Christ is seated at the right hand of God. Set your minds on things above, not on earthly things." We aren't of this world and don't act (at least we shouldn't act) like ungodly, worldly people. So we shouldn't be surprised when unbelievers act like unbelievers—their values are of this world and not heavenly at all. Still, when we were like that, Jesus loved us, and that's the way we have to be. We have to love those who judge us the same way Jesus does.

So what should you do? Press on and love them anyway. **LOVE THEM.** No matter what they throw your way, you're His. And because you belong to God, He's got your back, and therefore you can do what seems impossible—you can actually show love toward the people who show you no love at all. Now isn't that AWESOME! Like Jesus, who died for us while we were still sinners, through His power and life in us, we can show love to those who sin against us—toward those who judge us. When we do this we reflect Jesus! It may not be easy, but it's absolutely worth it!

Sweet Truth

You see, at just the right time, when we were still powerless, Christ died for the ungodly. Very rarely will anyone die for a righteous man, though for a good man someone might possibly dare to die. But God demonstrates His own love for us in this: While we were still sinners, Christ died for us. —Romans 5:6–8

Just Cool

Here's an idea...you probably watch some TV during the week, right? A typical half-hour TV show is twenty-two minutes without commercials. How about if you spent one show a week praying during commercials? That would be eight minutes in prayer. You could dedicate it to a specific friend or your enemies (I know it's hard)— like people who make fun of you or tease you because you're a Christian, or just people at school that you know for a fact don't know God. Maybe even write your prayers in a journal to keep track of them. Just think, by the end of the month you will have spent an extra thirty-two minutes in prayer for the very people that you least want to pray for. Let us know how it goes.

 How can I hear what God has to say to me? I've been trying to hear Him, but I can't. What should I do? —*Haylee*

Cam: A lot of people, including me, ask this question. I think we all have so much to learn about hearing from God, but I can share a couple of things that have helped me. First of all—**YOU CAN HEAR HIM!** So the first thing you're going to do is tell yourself what I just said. Go ahead, say it. "I can hear from God!"

How do I know that this is true? Well, I know that God has spoken and continues to speak to us through His Word—the Bible. Whatever God says in His Word will match up with the way He is going to lead you and speak into your life; it won't contradict what the Bible says or be different.

Reading and understanding the Scriptures is a great way to not just know about God, but to know Him personally as well, because the Bible is more than a book. I think Hebrews 4:12 kind of explains this when it says, "For the word of God is alive and active. Sharper than any double-edged sword, it penetrates even to dividing soul and spirit, joints and marrow; it judges the thoughts and attitudes of the heart." The Bible guides us on how to live for God day by day. So many times when I'm in tough or confusing situations, the Lord will bring a verse to my mind that will help me make the right decision.

Maybe you wish that God would just come and sit right next to you on your living room couch. Wouldn't that be amazing? Seriously, I don't think we could handle His brightness—His glory. We would be so overwhelmed by Him that we would just fall apart or scream or start dancing or something.

Erin: My mom gave me this quote: "Knowing the Bible is one thing. Knowing its Author is another." So true! We can read the Bible every day, but if we don't know—meaning, really get to know the One who wrote it—it's the same as if we never read it at all. Hmm. Back to your question.

For sure the will of God is revealed through the Word of God. One thing I can share is how I used to get confused by the many times

> **The more you get to know the Master or Good Shepherd, the better you'll know His voice.**

people heard the audible voice of God in the Bible. I thought that maybe I was like a second-class Christian, not spiritual enough or that something was wrong with me, because God didn't speak to me out loud. But I've talked to a lot of mature believers that I really respect who have never heard God's voice with their ears. What they have heard though, is God's voice in their hearts, and that is something we learn to recognize over time—I'm still learning and listening.

It's kind of like a mother can tell that her baby is crying in a room full of hundreds of babies, or like a dog can hear his master's voice in a crowd of people and come running to him. Jesus actually talks about what I'm trying to say when He referred to us (His followers, God's children) as sheep. Hopefully, the **Sweet Truths** we share will make more sense because of what we've already talked about.

The bottom line is, the more you get to know the Master or Good Shepherd, the better you'll know His voice. When you read and follow what the Bible tells you, you're listening to God's voice, and if you're following His Word, you're hearing and following Him.

 **The sheep hear His voice, and He calls His own sheep by name and leads them out. When He has brought out all His own, He goes before them, and the sheep follow Him, for they know His voice.** —John 10:3–4 (ESV)

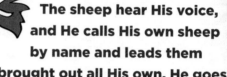

 **I am the good shepherd. I know my own and my own know me, just as the Father knows me and I know the Father; and I lay down my life for the sheep. And I have other sheep that are not of this fold. I must bring them also, and they will listen to my voice. So there will be one flock, one shepherd.** —John 10:14–16 (ESV)

I hear people say, "Wait on God. His timing is perfect." What does this even mean, and how am I supposed to know how long to wait for God? —Isabella Joy

Cam: Oh boy...okay, Erin is going to have to handle this one. I'm so not the person to ask about waiting...especially on God. My mother often says (and when I say "often" I mean, like, she says this all the time), "One day at a time. One prayer at a time. All in His perfect timing."

Even though I'm not very good at waiting, I want to answer you, so here's my best understanding. God is God. He knows everything, and His plans for you are absolutely perfect. It's like He already wrote your story and you're just living it out one day at a time. To wait on God is to trust Him. To trust that His timing for everything, including the little things, is perfect. As far as how long to wait, well...as long as it takes.

Erin: When I think about your question, I think about my brother, Hunter. We prayed and prayed for him to be healed. It seemed like we never stopped praying and waiting for God to do what only He could do. I say this because

I think prayer and waiting go hand in hand. In fact, I think our waiting should always be wrapped up in prayer.

If we're waiting on God, it's usually because we need Him to do something. But the crazy thing is, while we wait for God to move, He's already doing a work in our hearts. Sometimes it's not the answer but what happens in your heart during the waiting that matters.

Let me say this a different way. We wait on God for an answer to something we've been praying about...but what if the answer happens as we wait? So the answer isn't really the answer at all, it's what we learn about God while we wait on Him. Okay, WOW, that was maybe a little deeper than even I can understand.

Maybe you're praying for a friend to come to faith in Jesus, or a family member to be healed, whatever it is, God is working it all out, every detail, according to His plan. The **Sweet Truth** tells us to "be strong and take heart." Why? Because, let's face it, waiting isn't easy. So be encouraged and trust God... one minute at a time.

To wait on God is to trust Him.

Sweet Truth

Wait for the LORD; be strong and take heart and wait for the LORD.
—Psalm 27:14

Okay, so waiting patiently—like when you put a puzzle together and it takes time. Which is why I'm not the first one to grab a puzzle when the family is doing game night. For sure life can be a puzzle, and we really can't see the big picture the way God does. He makes lots of decisions we can't understand this side of eternity—decisions that sometimes don't fit together with our view of the way we think life should be. So try this: Get a puzzle, you know, one that isn't too hard to put together. Now turn all the pieces over so all you see is the plain back of the puzzle and put it together the best you can. That's how life is for us. We can't see the picture the way God does; He sees it all from eternity like a complete puzzle—breathtaking and beautiful. That's how He makes His decisions—based on our eternal good in His perfect timing as He puts the pieces of our life together.

Remember, a single piece of that puzzle isn't going to tell us much, other than we have to trust the Lord! But as we learn to see with an eternal perspective, it all becomes clearer. In fact, it becomes...well, just...just cool. Why not do this: carry around a random puzzle piece for a week to remind you that Jesus is Lord of the puzzle that life can seem to be sometimes!

I want to give up. I'm sick of the struggle. No one would even care if I disappeared anyway. What can I do with these feelings of hopelessness? —*hurting girl*

Cam: Listen, I'll come over right now. Seriously, I wish I could come to wherever you are so I could give you a hug. **DON'T GIVE UP!** Help and hope are on the way. How do I know? Because they're only a prayer away. GO TO GOD with your feelings, fears, struggles... everything. He promises to help us if we come to Him. Jesus said very clearly, "So I say to you: Ask and it will be given to you; seek and you will find; knock and the door will be opened to you. For everyone who asks receives; he who seeks finds; and to him who knocks, the door will be opened" (Luke 11:9–10).

And one more thing...YES, there are people in your life who would care if you disappeared. Besides, you can't actually disappear because God sees you. You can't hide from Him, nor should you ever want to.

Erin: Here's the deal: It's okay to give up as long as you GIVE IN to God. It's okay to struggle as long as your struggle leads you to your Savior. Hopelessness should lead you to the Author of all Hope. God looks down from heaven, and He sees you. He knows how you feel right now, and more than anything He wants to rescue you. He knows exactly what you're struggling with, and the crazy thing is...He's going to use it for your good.

God would never allow you to feel so low if He didn't have a plan in place to bring you up out of the darkness and into His marvelous light.

> God looks down from heaven, and He sees you.

Sweet Truth

"For I know the plans I have for you," declares the LORD, "plans to prosper you and not to harm you, plans to give you hope and a future. Then you will call upon me and come and pray to me, and I will listen to you. You will seek me and find me when you seek me with all your heart. I will be found by you," declares the LORD.
—Jeremiah 29:11–14a

Sometimes one of the best ways to deal with discouragement and hopelessness in your life is to try to encourage and bring hope to someone else. Anyone can bring an encouraging word to another! How about setting a goal of writing one anonymous note a week, just a few sentences—maybe include a Bible verse that's meaningful to you and explain why. Encourage someone you may not even meet until you get to heaven—some people call them "strangers," but I don't. Then pray over it and let the Lord lead you where to place it. Maybe you'll pick an address from the phone book and mail it, or slip it into a locker at school, or even leave it in a public restroom. But no one can resist reading a letter—it's a GREAT way to share God's love and witness to someone. Just remember to pray before you write each letter, and by the end of the year, you'll have left fifty-two encouraging letters. I have a good feeling that all of this encouraging you'll be doing is going to overflow in your life too!

My parents are always fighting. What should I do? They almost got divorced once! —*brady*

Cam: I'm so sorry about your parents' relationship being so difficult—I know how hard that can be. My parents went through a really rough time for a while, but God did the impossible. He brought my mom and dad back together, strengthened their marriage, and saved our family. So be encouraged, friend, it's not impossible, because we went through some pretty tough times and thankfully came out closer to God and each other.

But I know how you feel. It's sad and scary because you feel like everything is falling apart. When your parents are falling apart, it affects everyone and everything. Only God knows what your parents' choices will ultimately be, but you have every reason to hope, because the Lord's perfect plan is for them to keep the promises they made when they got married. Just continue to pray constantly, love them, and be a godly example. Oh and again, God can do the impossible!

Erin: I have a word for you, it's the word "almost"! Your parents ALMOST got divorced but didn't, and that is a huge step in the right direction. We sometimes automatically think the worst is going to happen. But if God is involved, the better than best is always possible. Right?! Rejoice that even though the road may be rocky, they're still together. Pray, pray, and pray some more. Pray first and foremost that your parents will seek God together. Ask the Lord to help

No matter what your circumstances are, God wants you to pray, give thanks, and be joyful.

your parents grow stronger in their relationship with Him first and with each other. Everything we need is found in Christ. Ya know what? Also pray that they will fall in love all over again.

I don't mean to sound like I'm forgetting about your struggle; it's hard, really hard. Sometimes I'm sure you feel absolutely helpless. We understand and know what it's like. But if you're praying and trusting God to do what only He can—you're not hopeless or helpless. You have Almighty God on your side. He's bending down from heaven to listen to your cries for help on behalf of your parents and family.

One more quick but very important thing. I've learned that love is a lot of hard work by watching my parents work out their problems. But anything worth fighting for is worth the fight! Still, you have to hang on to hope because your parents are pressing onward. And whatever you do, don't forget that just because they're having problems doesn't mean that they've stopped loving you. Here's a great **Sweet Truth** because no matter what your circumstances are, God wants you to pray, give thanks, and be joyful. I know it's hard, but if you seek Him, He will help you as you trust Him with everything that your family is going through.

Sweet Truth **Be joyful always; pray continually; give thanks in all circumstances, for this is God's will for you in Christ Jesus.**
—1 Thessalonians 5:16–18

I've tried to read the Bible, but it doesn't make sense. I've asked my mom to explain it to me, but she doesn't understand it either. What should I do? —*ella bell*

Cam: First of all, I'm so excited that you're trying to read the Bible, because some people don't even try. And I actually think I have the perfect answer for you. If you want to understand the Bible, you need to talk to the Author. Oh yeah! Before you even open it up, or maybe I should say every time you open it up, ask God to help you to know Him better. When you get to know Him more and more, He will help you understand what He wants you to know about Himself and everything else through what He has written in His Word. Here's the deal. You're not reading the Bible just to know what it says. You're reading the Bible so you can know—and I mean *really* know—the Author.

You can also talk with someone who understands the Bible. If you don't know anyone who reads the Bible, you can always talk with someone at your church. My last bit of advice is to get involved in a youth group so you can be taught God's Word. Oh, and don't forget, it's good to ask questions because that's how you learn.

Erin: I have a few things to add that might help you. First, be sure you have an accurate but contemporary translation of the Bible like the New International Version. Because there are many different versions or translations, be sure yours is a version you can understand. We like to use the NIV (New International Version 1984) but you might find that a different version works for you. Also, be sure the church or youth group you get involved with believes

> If you want to understand the Bible, you need to talk to the Author.

that the Bible is the Word of God, written by God *through* men, not *by* men (2 Peter 1:21). Also, pray before you read and ask God to open your mind and heart so you can understand, listen, and learn. I would start in the New Testament with one of the Gospels (Matthew, Mark, Luke, and John)—I especially like the Gospel of John.

Another thing, and I hope this encourages you, God wants you to know Him. He also wants you to know who you are and how to live your life. If you seek God through His Word, He WILL reveal Himself to you. No, you're not going to fully understand everything, but God will help you understand what you need to know when you need to know it.

Oh...and one more **REALLY IMPORTANT** thing. Jesus told us that the Holy Spirit would help us to understand what we need to know about God. Check out the **Sweet Truth**. You're not on your own, girl...the Holy Spirit will help you. ☺ I don't know about you, but having God on my side makes all the difference.

Sweet Truth

These things I have spoken to you while I am still with you. But the Helper, the Holy Spirit, whom the Father will send

in my name, He will teach you all things and bring to your remembrance all that I have said to you.
—John 14:25–26 (ESV)

Erin and I have been reading the Bible for a while. Of course you never stop learning, but maybe we can help you. Check out this **Cam Clip** if you're interested in getting into God's AMAZING WORD!

CAM CLIPS CODE: BIBLE 411

I'm afraid of everyone in my life dying. Thinking about it makes me cry. I don't want to tell anyone that I'm scared, but I need to talk about it because it bothers me so much. Help! —*leaha*

Cam: Ugh, well this breaks my heart. You might know this already, but my brother is in heaven. God brought him there when I was just six years old. I don't remember everything, but I can tell you that losing my brother has changed my life. I'm sorry you're feeling afraid, but trust me, I really do understand. The death of those we love and care about is something we all have to face in this life. And as much as we don't want to think about it or talk about it, death happens to everyone at some point.

But there's good news, and I mean really **GOOD NEWS**—Jesus defeated death! Check out Revelation 1:18: "I am the Living One; I was dead, and now look, I am alive for ever and ever! And I hold the keys of death and Hades." YES! Because of Jesus, and what He did for us, we will live forever. Did I just say "forever"? Yes, **F. O. R. E. V. E. R.** Who can even understand this? I don't know, because just thinking about living forever freaks me out.

John 3:16 says, "For God so loved the world that He gave his one and only Son, that whoever believes in Him shall not perish but have eternal life." We can rest in the love God has for us, live out His plan for our lives, and trust Him when it comes to death. It sounds so easy, but fear is real and it gets in the way of trusting God sometimes. In those moments of fear and doubt, that's when we need to remember the truth. And for me, the truth is I know that

"I don't know what the future holds, but I know Who holds the future."

because of Jesus, I will see my brother again! Knowing that my forever is safe with God helps me to live and trust Him today.

Erin: Okay, here's some big sister advice…you can't spend your life worrying about losing those you love or you'll never really live the life God has called you to live—you'll be too focused on the fear instead of loving every minute with the people God has placed in your life.

I would encourage you to really trust God. There's a quote I've heard many times: "I don't know what the future holds, but I know Who holds the future." No matter what we go through, God is still sovereign and good! One of my favorite verses is Romans 8:28: "And we know that in all things God works for the good of those who love him, who have been called according to his purpose." I have my own version of this: "It's all good!" Or as my dad often says, "It is what it is."

We don't get to go around life, only through it—good and bad, ups and downs. But as we do, we know that we're never alone. Take your fears and everything on your heart and mind right now and give it to God. Talk to Him. Pray! Journal. Do whatever it is that you do so you can give all of this to God.

Sweet Truth **Give your entire attention to what God is doing right now, and don't get worked up about what may or may not happen tomorrow. God will help you deal with whatever hard things come up when the time comes.**
—Matthew 6:34 *(The Message)*

Some people are obviously gifted, like they can sing or dance or whatever. I don't feel gifted at all. Did God forget about me? *—Julia*

Cam: GIRL...First things first: God NEVER forgets about ANYBODY—including you! So I was thinking about this, and it hit me that if we try to define what being gifted is based on what our friends or other people think, or maybe based on things that make us successful in the eyes of the world, we'll miss out and misunderstand.

Gifts are given for one reason—to glorify God and build up His kingdom. (Wait, maybe that's two reasons—LOL—but sort of one in my mind. Oh boy!) A gift can be singing and dancing (actually, I think these two are more like talents), like you said, or speaking, writing, math (that would not be me), serving, praying, and on and on the list goes...The important thing to focus on when looking for your own unique gifting is how you can use it to glorify God.

Erin: Absolutely—and actually, the Bible talks about other kinds of gifts as well called spiritual gifts. Spiritual gifts (1 Corinthians 12:4–11) include things like the word of knowledge, the gift of healing, as well as many others. You might have one or more of these gifts and as you get closer and deeper into the heart of God, it will become clear! Because you are a child of the King, you are gifted! In the end though, no matter what gifts we have—from highly visible things like singing, preaching, and dancing to behind-the-scenes things such as compassion or caring for the sick—without love, none of it matters. Because the greatest and most important thing about your gifts is that they are wrapped up and displayed with love. Love is the greatest gift you can give. And it's the one gift that keeps on giving! God is so good!

Love is the greatest gift you can give.

So, no matter what I say, what I believe, and what I do, I'm bankrupt without love. —1 Corinthians 13:3 *(The Message)*

My brother is a Marine, and he's going to another country. I won't be able to talk to him for a really long time. How will I know he's safe? —*marissa*

Cam: I'm so grateful for people like your brother. Men and women who serve our country and God by putting everything, even their lives, on the line to keep us safe from harm. When you do talk to him, please tell him that the Kelly family says thank you. I can appreciate your concern and fear for his safety; he's your brother. The good news is that God is right there with him, and Jesus Himself is interceding for him. He loves your brother and will watch over him.

Remember the story of David and Goliath? God protected young David from a giant who had been a warrior from his youth (1 Samuel 17). Trust Him to watch over your brother and pray for him as much as you can. In fact, we're going to pray for our military together, but first let's hear what Erin has to say.

Erin: Because no one knows what tomorrow holds, you have to rest in the reality that God knows and loves your brother. War is a terrible thing, yet it is a reality of life we all have to endure to some degree. I would say to do all you can to join hearts with your brother from afar. Write him often, pray for him, read the Bible, and find verses you can stand on.

The safest place in the world is in the center of God's will. So let's trust that your brother is right where God wants him to be, doing exactly what He has called him to do! Psalm 25:1–3 says, "In you, LORD my God, I put my trust. I trust in you; do not let me be put to shame, nor let my enemies triumph over me. No one who hopes in you will ever be put to shame, but shame will come on those who are treacherous without cause." Trust God with your brother and the enemies he will face.

The safest place in the world is in the center of God's will.

Sweet Truth

"The LORD himself goes before you and will be with you; he will never leave you nor forsake you. Do not be afraid; do not be discouraged." —Deuteronomy 31:8

I just had a really great idea. Let's take some time right now to pray for our military. Erin and I will lead. Let's go!

CAM CLIPS CODE: MILITARY

We were just thinking that maybe you can take some verses and put your brother's (or whoever you know that is serving in the military right now) name into the verse and pray what it says. We will get you started with the **Sweet Truth** verse, then you can look up the other verses and create your own prayer. The name we're going to put in for this is "Jonathan" because he's a real boy who is training to go into the Navy someday. Oh, and at the end of the verse praying, let's pray again for our military and our country.

> ### Deuteronomy 31:8
>
> The LORD Himself goes before Jonathan and will be with Him; He will never leave Jonathan nor forsake Him. Please help Jonathan to not be afraid, to not be discouraged.
>
> ### Deuteronomy 31:6
>
> ### Exodus 14:14
>
> ### Psalms 121:5–8

Why do some people have a lot of money and others don't? If I don't have a lot of money, does that mean that God has chosen not to bless me? I'm confused. —Melinda

Cam: We've never been asked this question before, so this should be very interesting. Before I share, I must say that everything we have is from God. Even the air we breathe is a gift from Him. First, maybe we should talk about what a blessing really is, I mean in God's eyes, and I'm pretty sure money isn't at the top of the list. I sort of think that ANYTHING that brings you closer to the Lord is a blessing.

As far as money goes, Jesus wanted us to know what's most important. He said, "No one can serve two masters. Either you will hate the one and love the other, or you will be devoted to the one and despise the other. You cannot serve both God and money" (Luke 16:13). No, obviously money isn't bad. We need money to live. We need money so we can give too. What's not good is putting anything before God—and in this verse Jesus is talking about loving money more than you love God. Let's find out what Erin thinks about all of this.

Erin: When I read this question, I immediately thought about two people in my life. One, a friend I grew up with who traveled to Africa on a few missions trips. I'll never forget what he said about his experience that rocked his world more than anything. He said, "It's challenging to visit the homes and hear the stories of these amazing people. What always blows my mind is the joy and true contentment that fills them, even though they're so materially poor." I personally experienced something very similar to this when I traveled to the Dominican Republic during my senior year in high school. I was completely overwhelmed by the joy I witnessed in the lives of the people who had nothing. The crazy thing is that they had nothing to give us (as far as money or material things) yet they shared their love, and that meant more than anything. These people had very little money and very few possessions, but they were rich in their relationship with God. And because they were rich in Christ, they freely shared all they had. Amazing! Now THAT'S what I would call being blessed and being a blessing!

Another very special person I thought of when I read this question is a sweet, beautiful little girl named Karis. She has a fatal disease (like my brother, Hunter, did) that steals from her daily. In fact, every single minute of every day she fights to live. Money and the things of this world mean absolutely

Bottom line, the greatest blessing is always Jesus.

nothing to Karis because she's just thankful to be alive. Life is the greatest gift to this precious little girl, and joy radiates from her because she's not caught up in the pursuit of worldly treasures.

So, all that to say, if it doesn't bring you closer to Jesus, it's not a blessing—whether it's money or miracles.

Jesus actually pointed to true riches not even being of this present world. In the Sermon on the Mount He took a look at this life and said very plainly, "Do not store up for yourselves treasures on earth, where moth and rust destroy, and where thieves break in and steal. But store up for yourselves treasures in heaven, where moth and rust do not destroy, and where thieves do not break in and steal. For where your treasure is, there your heart will be also" (Matthew 6:19–21).

Bottom line, the greatest blessing is always Jesus.

Sweet Truth **Lust for money brings trouble and nothing but trouble. Going down that path, some lose their footing in the faith completely and live to regret it bitterly ever after.**
—1 Timothy 6:10 *(The Message)*

What do you do when you're being backtalked? Like, no matter what you say, your friend always has a better answer? *—unicorn lover*

Cam: I know what you mean, because although I hate to admit it I sometimes think of my best comebacks after the fact instead of right when I need to. But when you think about it, life isn't about being able to prove yourself; it's about loving God and sharing Jesus.

Jesus wants us to be like Him, to love people, including people that backtalk and think they're always right. I don't know what it is, maybe sin, but I can relate to being on both sides of this question. It's weird, because sometimes I just want to be right and so I have a comeback to whatever just so I can get the last word. It's not like I'm thinking about it in this way; it just happens. And then other times I've been on the other end of things, where it's like someone has to say something and no matter what I say, she knows more. Why do we do this to each other? It's so ridiculous. Like who cares who is right or wrong, let's just all get along. Oh yeah—that rhymes.

I think the best thing to do in these types of situations is to not get into it—it really does take two and if you refuse to participate then

> When we pray, trust Him, and live the way He has called us to live, it changes everything.

it's harder for her to keep the game going. How about this: The next time this happens, if you can, say a quick prayer, maybe a silent one if you can't walk away and pray. Seriously, God will help you respond, and like I just said, the best response just might be to not say anything— but pray.

Erin: I agree, **PRAY**! When we refuse to respond in the same way, and instead respond in the opposite spirit, like Jesus would, it's very powerful. Remember, you can't control what your friend will say or do; in fact, you can't control anything but your response. You can decide, even before it happens, to do what you think Jesus would want you to do. You know for sure that He would always want you to do all things in LOVE—because love covers over a multitude of sins. What does that mean? Well, when we treat others (especially the people who drive us crazy) with love, we defeat the power of the enemy in that situation. The enemy wants to destroy relationships, but Jesus wants to build them up, make them stronger. When we pray, trust Him, and live the way He has called us to live, it changes everything...and maybe, just maybe, your friend will see Jesus in you and she'll change too.

Sweet Truth

Above all, love each other deeply, because love covers over a multitude of sins. —1 Peter 4:8

A girl at school is so mean to me. I tried talking to her, but she totally ignored me and acted as if I were invisible. She is ruining my life. —*myah800*

Cam: Okay, I'm just going to have to come to your school and have a talk with this girl. Hmm, that's my initial reaction to your situation. But I'm pretty sure that getting in this girl's business would not help you at all. I've heard it said before that "hurt people, hurt people." In other words, this girl is probably mean to you because someone is or was mean to her. Maybe she was hurt so badly at some point that now she protects her heart by being mean to others. It doesn't make sense, but it could be true. Regardless, God always wants us to take the way of love. It's not easy to be kind, loving, and gracious when someone is mean and rude, but that's why you need Jesus. We can't do the right thing, the hard things, in life without Him. WE NEED JESUS! Not just sometimes, but all the time.

Erin: You're not invisible! Let's start with the fact that no matter how someone treats you, you need to remember who you are and to WHOM you belong. You're a child of the One True King. You belong to Him. He sees you and loves you so much more than you'll ever be able to comprehend. The more you know God, the more you understand, know, and live out who you are. When you know Him, you're able to respond to difficult situations the way He would want you to respond. Not only that, you're able to hold your head up with God confidence because you know that no matter what people or life might throw at you, God loves you and He'll fight for you.

One more thing. Don't give this girl the power to ruin your life. Seriously, you belong to Jesus, the All-Powerful Ruler of the universe. This girl has absolutely no power over you unless you

> No matter how someone treats you—you need to remember who you are and to WHOM you belong. You're a child of the One True King.

give it to her. So… stop giving it to her. Fix your heart, mind, and everything on Jesus. I promise if you do this, you'll be amazed by how you respond to her with love the next time.

Oh, and one more very important thing…pray for her. I know, I know, why should you pray for someone who treats you so badly? Well, that's exactly why you should pray for her. If she belonged to Jesus, she wouldn't act the way she does (or at least you would hope she wouldn't), so pray for her to come to faith in Christ. In fact, let's get crazy bold and pray that God would use you to speak into her life—through your words but even more so through the way you treat her with love. WOW!

SUPER LOOOOOOOONG

Sweet Truth

"I'm telling you to love your enemies. Let them bring out the best in you, not the worst. When someone gives you a hard time, respond with the energies of prayer, for then you are working out of your true selves, your God-created selves. This is what God does. He gives His best—the sun to warm and the rain to nourish—to everyone, regardless: the good and bad, the nice and nasty. If all you do is love the lovable, do you expect a bonus? Anybody can do that.... In a word, what I'm saying is, *grow up*. You're kingdom subjects. Now live like it. Live out your God-created identity. Live generously and graciously toward others, the way God lives toward you."

—Matthew 5:44–48 *(The Message)*

Just Cool

We talked about praying, so let's do it. Pray for the people in your life who do not know God. Maybe there are kids at school or in your neighborhood or wherever—you know they need Jesus, so pray for them. Right here. Right now. And don't stop! Keep on praying until you see God move in their lives.

Dear Jesus . . .

I always care what people think of me. I try to please everyone and just end up being miserable while they all seem to go about life all happy. Ugh. What am I supposed to do? *—reesa*

Cam: Well, as a preteen, teenager, or any other age for that matter, we all seem to care about what other people think of us. I guess it's just the way it is, or maybe the way we've made it to be. But here's the deal: We should never care more about what people think of us than what God thinks of us. Because what He thinks is ultimately all that matters. I like the way Luke 9:25 says this: "What good is it for someone to gain the whole world, and yet lose or forfeit their very self?" If you had everything but God, in the end you have nothing and lose your "very self." So what you're supposed to do is concentrate on pleasing God and caring about what He thinks of you. Matthew 6:33 tells us, "But seek first His kingdom and His righteousness, and all these things will be given to you as well." If you make pleasing God your first priority, He will move things to fall into place, but if you put pleasing others above God, then, well, you'll probably just end up being miserable.

Erin: Obviously you don't want to be miserable, right? My guess is that you're sick and tired of trying to please everyone. I hear you loud and clear, girl. Bottom line about the pleasing-people thing— you can't please everyone all the time. You might be able to please some people most of the time, but not everyone, every time. And guess what? You're not meant to. You were not created to be a people pleaser. God made you because He delights in you and longs for you to please Him, to re-

> You were not created to be a people pleaser. God made you because He delights in you and longs for you to please Him, to reflect His love.

flect His love. What pleases God the most is your faith in Him and love for Him and others.

Again, you can't please everyone. Just thinking about this makes me cringe because I get it. You don't want to rock the boat—I hear you. You think if you can just do right by everybody then things will roll along smoothly for you. It's impossible. People are people and no matter how hard you try, you can't make everyone happy. God is the giver of all good things. He's the only one that can fill our hearts. Give yourself a break, my friend. Stop trying to please people and just fix your eyes on Jesus and rest in the truth that you are loved right now more than you can imagine. Surrender this need you have to be all things to all people to the great, All-Powerful, All-Knowing, Almighty God.

Keep your eyes on *Jesus*, who both began and finished this race we're in. Study how He did it. Because He never lost sight of where He was headed—that exhilarating finish in and with God—He could put up with anything along the way: Cross, shame, whatever. And now He's *there*, in the place of honor, right alongside God. —Hebrews 12:2 *(The Message)*

Sometimes I get this urge to do something that isn't Christianlike. What do I do? It's too hard. *—Kenna*

Cam: Hey, I can totally relate because I get tempted to do things I know I'm not supposed to do sometimes and it's hard...so hard. Temptation is part of life, and you can do one of two things: give in and fall for the temptation or call on Jesus for the grace to overcome the temptation. The Apostle Paul said, "No temptation has overtaken you except what is common to mankind. And God is faithful; He will not let you be tempted beyond what you can bear. But when you are tempted, He will also provide a way out so that you can endure it" (1 Corinthians 10:13). That truth helps me to know that God is faithful and won't allow me to be tempted beyond what I can handle.

Erin: You're not alone. I'm pretty sure every person who has ever lived has struggled with this, even the people we think are super Christians—they struggle too. Just read the Bible—the evidence is written all throughout Scripture. Please be encouraged because we all go through times when the temptation to do something we know is wrong gets really hard to resist—it's part of being human. It's part of why we desperately need a Savior!

I try to remember that where there is temptation, there is a tempter, and I'm being set up. Paul also shared something cool that the Lord said to him in 2 Corinthians 12:9: "But He said to me, 'My grace is sufficient for you, for my power is made perfect in weakness.'" Even though we're weak, it's through our weaknesses that God's power is made perfect. Two quick things: First, cry out honestly to God about the temptation you face; He responds to honesty and sincerity. And second, if you do fall, get back up. Repent, confess your sin, and move on in the Lord. Don't get down on yourself with failure; learn from it and make it work for you. His grace truly is sufficient. All the time. Every time!

Even though we're weak, it's through our weaknesses that God's power is made perfect.

No test or temptation that comes your way is beyond the course of what others have had to face. All you need to remember is that God will never let you down; He'll never let you be pushed past your limit; He'll always be there to help you come through it.

—1 Corinthians 10:13 *(The Message)*

GETTING DOWN TO BUSINESS: Okay, if you're being tempted right now, let's talk about it. RIGHT NOW. Write it down. Get it out and then let God take care of it. After you write it all out, look up and write down this verse: 2 Corinthians 12:9. We'll get you started.

But he said to me, "My grace...

What's the difference between joy and happiness? Aren't they like the same thing? —*Rachelle*

Cam: Now THIS is a cool question! Though they seem like they're the same, there's a huge difference between joy and happiness. Outwardly there are similarities, but joy and happiness are very different! I've said it before and I'll say it again—I'm not a theologian or Bible scholar (actually I'm no kind of scholar at all, except maybe a "hot-chocolate-ologist"), I'm just a girl like you and my Bible is no bigger than yours. (Unless you have one of those super-small adorable backpack Bibles, like maybe a pink or purple one.) Anyway, here's what I know: joy comes from heaven—it's a fruit of the Spirit.

Joy doesn't depend on situations that can change in a heartbeat. Romans 14:17 says, "For the kingdom of God is not a matter of eating and drinking, but of righteousness, peace and joy in the Holy Spirit." When it comes to joy, the Bible explains that it's part of the kingdom of God and kind of unrelated to eating and activities or life in general. I think it's obvious (at least to me ☺) that some foods, like brussels sprouts in my case, can make you feel unhappy. And if that's the case, then other foods—like pizza or barbecue chips—can make me feel really happy. But joy grows from within, and is not related to anything I wear, eat, buy, feel...you get the idea. It comes from the Spirit of God and isn't of this world. And the REALLY COOL thing is that nothing in this world gave JOY to me (because it comes from God), so nothing in this world can take it from me.

Erin: I love it! That's the amazing thing about joy—and all the rest of the fruit of the Spirit, really—it's planted in your heart by God as an expression of His eternal life and character, and nothing in time or this world can take it from you. NOTHING! There are many things that can make us happy—from a surprise visit from a friend who moved away to a sweet song by Justin Bieber (or your favorite artist, since of course we know that not all girls like JB's music). Happiness usually depends on what's happening in our lives, but joy depends on Jesus!

Happiness usually depends on what's happening in our lives, but joy depends on Jesus!

Joy takes root and becomes part of who we are; it's not here today and gone tomorrow. Instead, it's an attitude   and an outgrowth of the life of God as it's lived out through us. As we grow in Christ, the fruit of the Spirit slowly ripens in our hearts, producing His image. And as it does, one of the most beautiful traits is joy—joy that sees us through the good and bad times. Joy that carries us steadfastly through tears and tragedies as well as dreams and achievements, because it depends solely on the character and faithfulness of God.

 **But the fruit of the Spirit is love, joy, peace, patience, kindness, goodness, faithfulness, gentleness and self-control.**
—Galatians 5:22-23

Does God get disappointed with me when I doubt Him? —*Evalynn*

Cam: Ahh, this is such a great question because I think at some point in our lives we all doubt God. I think we usually doubt Him when things don't go how we had hoped or when something happens that is tragic and we don't understand why. The way I see it, God knows we're just human—He made us. He understands that we will only know and understand so much as we journey through life. Things are going to happen that will cause us to doubt His love. But in these moments or days or weeks or months of doubt we need to pray and remember that God's love is greater than our doubt. When I start to doubt God, I write verses down on index cards and carry them with me. When you're dealing with doubt it's easy to start believing lies—lies about who you are and who God is. That's why I need the truth. If I fill my mind with what's true, I find my way back to faith.

Erin: After reading this question, so many thoughts filled my mind. First of all, I thought about the men and women in the Bible...like David, Jeremiah, Peter, Thomas, Ruth, Esther, and so many others. We read about them and think they're superhuman, when really they're just like you and me. They needed Jesus just as much as you and I do. Although their stories give us examples of great faith, we also find that they struggled in the midst of their cir-

God's love is greater than all of our emotions, doubts, fears, and frustrations!

cumstances. That's why I love reading the Bible, because you not only learn about the triumphs of God's people, you also learn about their doubts, fears, and frustrations. They were real people. And God's Word gives us insight into their struggles so we can know that we're not alone in ours.

To answer your question...no, I don't think God gets disappointed when you doubt Him. Why do I think this? Well, I guess because I believe that God's love is greater than all of our emotions, doubts, fears, and frustrations. He dealt with our doubt by sending Jesus to take care of everything that would separate us from the Father. It's a done deal. You can choose to go on doubting, but His love for you will never change and He'll wait for you. I can just picture it all now...you surrendering your doubts one prayer at a time and God scooping you up into His loving arms, replacing your doubts and fears with greater love and faith. It's a beautiful sight!

Sweet Truth

This then is how we know we belong to the truth, and how we set our hearts at rest in his presence whenever our hearts condemn us. For God is greater than our hearts, and He knows everything. —1 John 3:19–20

Why does the Bible say not to fear, but it also tells us to fear God? I'm confused. —*Jillian*

Cam: That does sound confusing, and trust me, you're not the only person that's been confused about this. The more we think of God as a Father, the clearer that fear factor becomes. The Lord wants us to have confidence in His love for us, so He continually encourages us to face challenges with trust and faith. Isaiah 41:10 says, "So do not fear, for I am with you; do not be dismayed, for I am your God. I will strengthen you and help you; I will uphold you with my righteous right hand." And in Philippians 4:13 the Apostle Paul assures us that he was able to rely on God in very difficult circumstances, saying, "I can do all this through Him who gives me strength." So when it comes to facing the challenges of life, we are not to fear, but to trust God and bravely move forward.

On the other hand, the Bible is clear that our attitude toward God is not to be fear (like being afraid), but loving reverence. Psalm 33:18 (**Sweet Truth**) puts it this way: "But the eyes of the LORD are on those who fear him, on those whose hope is in his unfailing love." The Lord is looking to those who relate to Him with the respect He deserves and yet hope in His love. Okay, so "reverence" is a big

crazy word that basically means loyalty and devotion, and it's as if you're just like "wow" because of how great God is.

Erin: Oftentimes that word "fear" is really better translated "to revere" or "to be in awe of," like Cam tried to explain to you. Kind of the way we should relate to our earthly fathers. In a way the Bible is telling us to honor the Lord, respect and revere Him, both because He is all-powerful and because He loves us! And in that love and power, we can trust Him to stick up for us—to defend and fight for us when we're in trouble. He won't let us down because He loves us so much.

Our attitude toward God is not to be fear (like being afraid), but loving reverence.

But like our earthly fathers should, if He sees us making choices that will put us in harm's way, He'll step in and set us straight if necessary. In the end, He'll always do the most loving thing for us—even if it hurts. I love Romans 8:31. It says, "What, then, shall we say in response to these things? If God is for us, who can be against us?"

Sweet Truth

But the eyes of the LORD are on those who fear Him, on those whose hope is in His unfailing love. —Psalm 33:18

Do you actually think that one person can make a difference in this huge world? Like can I make a difference at all? —*Johanna*

Cam: Girl, you make a difference just by being alive, by being YOU! God made you! He has a purpose for your life, or you wouldn't be here. I think it's so cool that you want to make a difference, but remember, it's Jesus who ultimately makes the difference in people's lives and in this world. The amazing thing is, He set you apart because He wants you to be a part of

> God set you apart because He wants you to be a part of what He's doing on earth. He wants to use you! Awesome!

what He's doing on earth. He wants to use you! Awesome!

Think about it this way. Like dominoes—when you line them all up and knock down the first one, the rest of them fall down. When God moves you to do something good in this world on His behalf, like encourage a stranger or help someone in need or love your enemy (ouch—so hard!), what you do for people might move them to do something for someone else and so on, like falling dominoes. You never know—because of a simple act of kindness you could change a person's life and maybe even change the world.

Erin: I think sometimes we get this idea that to make a difference we have to be the president of the United States or someone in a position of great influence, like a celebrity. Here's the deal: You don't have to be famous or well known to make a difference. Simple acts of kindness that go completely unnoticed by most of the world DO NOT go unnoticed by God. He sees it all. He sees you. He knows your heart and your desire to make a difference. In fact, He placed that desire in you. Now that's COOL! Because of Christ in us, we want to affect people's lives for His glory. God will guide you into the good works He has already planned in advance for you to do.

One more thing that I think is actually the answer to this question and all others...when you love Jesus, you'll make a difference in this world. Jesus is the difference! When we love Him, we can't help but live for Him. Part of living for Him includes loving others—like everyone. If you want to make a difference, fall in love with Jesus and just watch how He uses you to change the world! Yeah!

Know that the LORD has set apart the godly for Himself; the LORD will hear when I call to Him. —Psalm 4:3

Let's talk to some people who have decided to make a difference in this world. I think after you watch this video you'll see how you can make a difference too. CHECK IT OUT!

ᔓCAM CLIPS CODE: MAKE A DIFFERENCE

I've always tried to be someone I'm not for people. I tried to be perfect, but now I don't know if they will accept me for who I really am. What do you think I should do? —*Emily*

Cam: I understand the pressure to want to be accepted, but the simple fact is that you've got to decide what's more important: being accepted by your friends or being accepted by Jesus. We've got to realize that He loves us for who we are, and we don't have to be someone else to try to impress Him—or anyone else, for that matter. I don't think it's ever right to try to be someone you're not. I think a lot of girls do this because they don't realize that in Jesus we have everything we need—most importantly acceptance. Jesus loves you just the way you really are, and you don't have to fake it with Him. What a relief! I think the best thing you can do is love Him—He won't let you down. And the more you know and love Him, the more comfortable you'll become with who you are and who He created you to be.

Erin: I really appreciate your honesty, admitting that you're trying to be someone you're not to win the hearts of other people. It takes courage to admit something like this, so be encouraged. First of all, I have to point out that the Lord loves you for who you are—period, end of story! I mean, He knows you from the inside out—and He loves you. You don't have to pretend with Jesus.

A true friend isn't going to want you to try to be someone you're not. A true friend will know you inside and out and still see you as precious. Some of my most favorite verses are in Psalm 139. These truths show us just how intimately God knows us and just how much we mean to Him. "For you created my inmost being; you knit me together in my mother's womb. I praise you because I am fearfully and wonderfully made; your works are wonderful, I know that full well. My frame was not hidden from you when I was made in the secret place, when I was woven together in the depths of the earth. Your eyes saw my unformed body; all the days ordained for me were written in your book before one of them came to be. How precious to me are your thoughts, God! How vast is the sum

> He knows you from the inside out—and He loves you. You don't have to pretend with Jesus.

of them!" (Psalm 139:13–17). You don't have to try to be perfect for Jesus; He loves you just the way you are.

Does God still perform miracles? —*Jenna*

Cam: YES! Yes, God still performs miracles today. How do I know? Well, because God is the same God who performed miracles in the Bible. If He hasn't changed, why would He stop doing what only He can do? Miracles, the way I understand them, are things that happen that could never happen unless God did them. When you think about it, life itself is a miracle. The fact that we can live and breathe on this planet is an example that God is still in the miracle business.

Another thing I was just thinking about is that

The fact that we can live and breathe on this planet is an example that God is still in the miracle business.

we don't always hear about the miraculous things God is doing. Unfortunately, all you ever hear about on television is bad news. From time to time there might be a story about a person surviving a plane crash or how some-one was diagnosed with cancer and given no hope, but then a few weeks later the can-cer was totally gone...these are miracles. Maybe we're too busy to see that miracles happen all around us. I think this might be a good thing to pray about...that God would open our eyes, ears, hearts, and minds to witness the miracles He's performing in our midst. After Erin shares, we'll pray. Okay?

Erin: It's interesting because whenever I think of or hear the word "miracle," I think of my brother, Hunter. It's crazy because Hunter was so sick and we prayed for him to be miraculously healed and he wasn't, but that doesn't mean that God didn't do the impossible. God did perform a miracle in the midst of Hunter's life by allowing his suffering to point to Jesus and His suffering

132

on behalf of all of us. Our family ended up being healed. Even though we were praying for a physical healing for Hunter, God instead gave us the greater healing that we all needed when He saved us and we put our faith and hope in Jesus.

 **He is the living God, world without end. His kingdom never falls. His rule continues eternally. He is a savior and rescuer. He performs astonishing miracles in heaven and on earth.** —Daniel 6:26-27 *(The Message)*

I made a really bad decision. Should I tell my parents? I'm afraid they'll ground me for like a year. —*Shay*

Cam: First I want to say how much I love the way you are right up front about that bad decision! Being honest about our mistakes is HUGE. So many people try to hide a bad decision so they can avoid taking responsibility for their actions.

"Should I tell my parents?" Um...well...I don't

know the whole deal with your circumstances, and it all seems like something you would rather hide—but a couple of Scriptures come to mind that may help you with this situation. First, Luke 6:31, the "Golden Rule," says you should, "Do to others as you would have them do to you." Flip this all around—if you were the parent, how would you want your son or daughter to handle it? Would you want him or her to be honest even if it was a horrible mistake? Treat your parents the same way you'd want to be treated. Any time you want to hide, you gotta stop and think, because there's only one place to hide: in the darkness! No one hides in the light, so you have to ask yourself why you might be trying to hide.

Another verse that my mother reminded me of for this is Proverbs 28:13. It's awesome: "He who conceals his sins does not prosper, but whoever confesses and renounces them finds mercy." My advice is to honor your parents and deal with it. Maybe you will get grounded for a year (oh my goodness, if this really happens, write to me at the HCWG website and I'll send you candy), but there are very few things that are as important as your relationship with your parents. Admit what happened, turn from your mistake, and trust

So go to God first, humble yourself, confess what you did, receive His forgiveness, and make it right.

that your parents will deal with it as they should.

Erin: There's a very powerful yet simple principle that echoes through the Bible because it reflects the heart and character of God Himself—honesty and truth. For example, 1 John 1:9 tells us, "If we confess our sins, He is faithful and just and will forgive us our sins and purify us from all unrighteousness." So absolutely you should tell your parents, particularly if this "really bad decision" breaks their rules, their hearts, and their trust in you. When you come clean you are demonstrating that your love relationship with them is worth any price you have to pay—even a year in your room—and that whatever you did to disrespect them wasn't worth it! It sounds like that decision you made was a sin against God first and foremost (since all sin is ultimately against Him). But it also sounds like you've hurt the two people who love you most in this world. So go to God first and then to your parents, humble yourself, confess what you did, receive His forgiveness, and make it right. We all make mistakes, and I'd be willing to bet your parents will go easier on you if you tell them than if they find out about this from someone else.

Sweet Truth

When I kept silent, my bones wasted away through my groaning all day long. For day and night Your hand was heavy upon me; my strength was sapped as in the heat of summer. Then I acknowledged my sin to You and did not cover up my iniquity. I said, "I will confess my transgressions to the LORD"—and You forgave the guilt of my sin. —Psalm 32:3–5

What should you do if you know that some of your friends are bad influences, but you can't seem to stop hanging out with them or you don't have the courage to say no? —*Say Say*

Cam: As I'm reading your question, it sounds like you actually know the answer, so I'm thinking that you already know what you should do. Maybe the real question is, how do you find the strength to live up to the light shining on the path you know you should follow? (Oh yeah, that last sentence was a good one!) 1 Corinthians 15:33 makes it pretty clear: "Do not be misled: 'Bad company corrupts good character.'" So the question is, what's worth more to you, hanging out with friends that you know will get between you and the Lord, or the approval of the Lord?

Another thing I'm thinking is that your courage will cause your friends to wonder about you. Initially they might make fun of you or be rude because you're not going along with them. But when they get in trouble or they finally realize that their choices are not good, they'll remember your strength. They'll remember that you chose what's right rather than what's popular. How cool would it be if your friends turn to you and ask how you're able to make good decisions and you get to tell them about Jesus!

Erin: The choice is very clear, for sure it demands courage, like you said, but the decision is even more basic. Luke 9:23–24 kind of puts it plainly: "Then He said to them all: 'If anyone would come after me, he must deny himself and take up his cross daily and follow me. For whoever wants to save his life will lose it, but whoever loses his life for me will save it.'" So really, will you deny yourself and the desire to hang with these bad influences that will get between you and the Lord?

Choose what's right rather than what's popular!

In a way, it's a question of who you will serve. Who do you love more—your friends (who are bad influences) or Jesus? I can't help but think of that verse from the book of Joshua when he stood at a similar crossroads and had to decide whom he would serve—the one true God or the gods of his time. He made up his mind and issued a challenge to those around him, a challenge that you might be able to relate to: "But if serving the LORD seems undesirable to you, then choose for yourselves this day whom you will serve, whether the gods your ancestors served beyond the Euphrates, or the gods of the Amorites, in whose land you are living. But as for me and my household, we will serve the LORD" (Joshua 24:15). We have this verse hanging up in our house to remind us that we have a choice. I've had to ask myself several times, and I guess you have to ask yourself too—as for you, who will you serve: your friends or Jesus? Because it's obvious that you can't serve both.

Sweet Truth

He who walks with the wise grows wise, but a companion of fools suffers harm. —Proverbs 13:20

Saying Good-Bye for Now...

*I*t seems that something like what we've been able to share together should never come to an end. It's just too awesome. But here we are.

It's that time.

God says in His Word in Ecclesiastes (where do these book names come from anyway?—seriously) that there is a time for everything under heaven. Let's read it together.

There is a time for everything, and a season for every activity under the heavens:
a time to be born and a time to die,
a time to plant and a time to uproot,
a time to kill and a time to heal,
a time to tear down and a time to build,
a time to weep and a time to laugh,

a time to mourn and a time to dance,

a time to scatter stones and a time to gather them,

a time to embrace and a time to refrain from embracing,

a time to search and a time to give up,

a time to keep and a time to throw away,

a time to tear and a time to mend,

a time to be silent and a time to speak,

a time to love and a time to hate,

a time for war and a time for peace,

a time to read HCWG DEVO #2 *and a time to pass it on and share it with your friends (especially the ones who don't know Jesus).*

—Ecclesiastes 3:1–8

Okay, okay, so the last three lines are NOT in the Bible. But it's in my heart and now it's written down—in this book that you're reading right now. Listen, if you keep all that you've learned from this experience to yourself—that would not be cool at all. Yes, all of this is for you, but it's also for you to share with your friends and family, and with the people that God has placed in your life. You see, more than anything Jesus wants us to love Him. When we love Him, we can't help but share Him. Taking what you've gained through this *HCWG* experience to wherever so others can know Jesus more—now that's what makes this journey together more than AWESOME and amazing. And just think, if you talk about *HCWG* with another girl and then she shares it with her friends, and then her friends share it with their families and friends…do you see it all unfolding? Like the ripple effect of what Jesus can do if we step out in faith to share what He has done in our lives.

I'm so excited I could scream. In fact, I'll be right back!

Oh yeah, a good, joy-filled scream is a must every once in a while. In fact, take a quick break right now and go for it. Scream! Just make sure you tell people so they don't freak out and think you like saw a spider or something. Eww, don't even get me started.

If God says there's a time for everything, I'm pretty sure He means there's a time for EVERYTHING. And right now is the time for us to say good-bye. But not only that, it's time for something BIG-TIME IMPORTANT. I know you're like, WHAT?

It's time for you to GO ALL IN for Jesus. It's time to take all of you and go ALL IN.

"What do you mean?" I know you pretty well by now, so I knew you would ask me that question. ☺

I mean…give your ALL to Jesus.

We've shared a lot, learned a lot, and hopefully changed a lot as a result of spending this time with God and one another. But this isn't the end of the story, even though we've come to the end of this book.

Your story is still being written. God is still at work in your heart and life. And I know for a fact that He wants all of you. I think some of us think it's okay to live for Jesus just some of the time. I know I need to give Him more of me for sure.

So let's end this HCWG devo by praying that God will help us to go ALL IN FOR HIM. And if we do, I just know that we will be filled with so much crazy joy that people will want what we have—they'll want Jesus—and that's the whole point.

Let's pray...

Heavenly Father...
You are amazing! We have so much to be thankful for, but first and most important we thank You for Jesus—Your One and Only Son. Thank You for loving us so much that You gave us Your Son so that we would have eternal life, joy, hope, peace, and everything else that we need for life and godliness. Thank You for helping us to know and love You more every day. Thank You for Your Word. Help us to long to spend time with You through reading the Bible...In Jesus' name we pray.

Wait, you might have more that You want to say to God, so go for it! Use this extra journal space to keep on praying. Oh, and really quick...we love You!